AMERICAN LOCOMOTIVES

A Pictorial Record of Steam Power

1900-1950

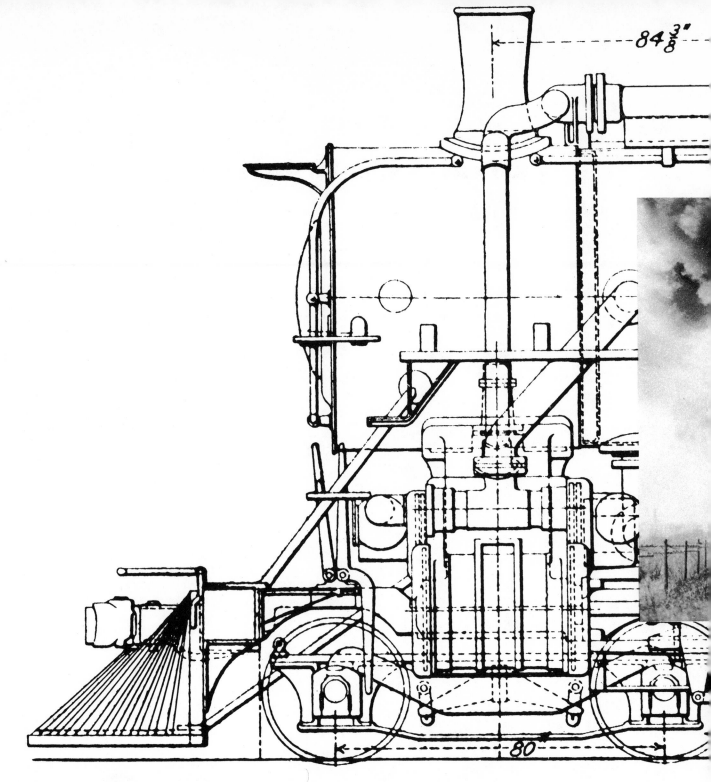

Books by Edwin P. Alexander: MODEL RAILROADS   ☆   IRON

HORSES: AMERICAN LOCOMOTIVES 1829-1900   ☆   AMERICAN

LOCOMOTIVES: A Pictorial Record of Steam Power 1900-1950   ☆   THE

PENNSYLVANIA RAILROAD: A Pictorial History

AMERICAN

Locomotives

A PICTORIAL RECORD OF STEAM POWER, 1900-1950

BY EDWIN P. ALEXANDER

BONANZA BOOKS · *New York*

Design and Typography
by Jos. Trautwein

PREFACE

THERE IS, OF COURSE, NO ACTUAL DIVIDING LINE BEtween the locomotives of the nineteenth and twentieth centuries. The development of the steam locomotive was spurred continually by the ever-increasing demand for more efficient power and speed as rolling equipment became heavier and more capacious. Today, as fifty years ago, designing and engineering work still goes on with its thoughts on the future, although other types of power are supplanting the conventional steam engine. Today, few railroads are without some diesel electric power and a number have already converted completely to it. Thus this summary of some representative motive power in the first half of the twentieth century may possibly be an epitaph of the steam locomotive we have been familiar with.

This book is really a continuation of the locomotive story begun with *Iron Horses*—carrying on where the former left off. Of course, the motive power pictured and described is only a minute portion of the tens of thousands of steel steeds which have kept the country's railroads ahead in efficiency, speed, and service. The locomotives illustrated have been chosen for their being either milestones in design, particularly representative of their railroad, or pictorially outstanding. Nearly every major system is represented, although in a few instances it was impossible to obtain certain information which would permit other engines to be shown. It should be understood, too, that this book, like its predecessor, is not intended to be technical, although it does include more mechanical data than the former and in most cases diagrams of the locomotives illustrated.

My sincere thanks are due the many railroad officers and those connected with locomotive building who have contributed to the contents in some form or other—so many, in fact, that to mention them here is impossible due to space limitations. I shall hope in appreciation that the motive power illustrated will sufficiently represent them or their railroads.

EDWIN P. ALEXANDER

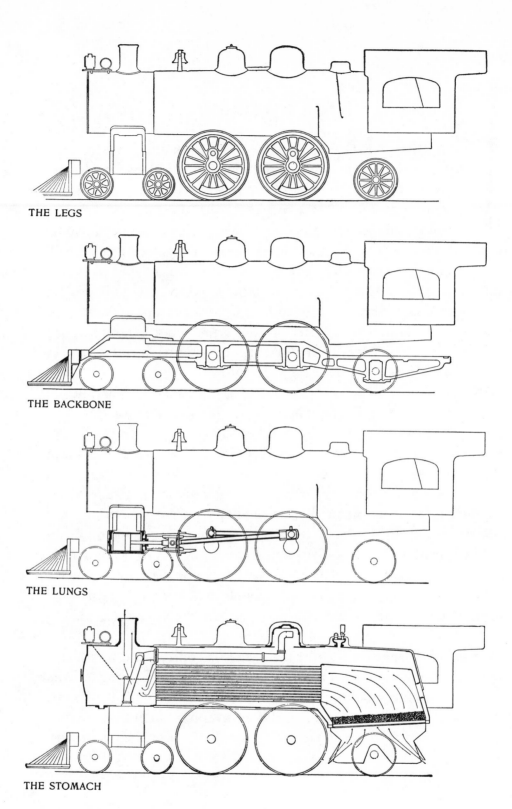

THE LEGS

THE BACKBONE

THE LUNGS

THE STOMACH

Anatomy of the locomotive 1901

AMERICAN LOCOMOTIVES

THE STEAM ERA IN RAILROADING IS PASSING – SLOWLY BUT subtly and surely another tractive force is displacing the thundering steel steeds with their smoke and steam and chime whistles. This new power—the diesel electric locomotive with its throbbing efficiency, streamlining, and air horn—has yet to create a similar tradition and capture the imagination as the steam engines did with their vibrant "alive" feeling. Of course, nostalgia fathers such thoughts; we hate to see familiar things disappear, but the cliché "Progress cannot be denied" is appropriate.

Steam locomotive partisans may take some consolation in the fact that it will probably be a generation at least before the last of these engines comes to the end of its track. In parts of the country, some railroads will continue to build their own steam locomotives for some years to come, but except for a national emergency, the last commercially built machine of this type for domestic use has now been delivered.

This threshold of the diesel age in railroading is, then, a particularly opportune time to look over the last fifty years of development of the steel steeds which have been the backbone of America's transportation system. Each of those illustrated and briefly described is fairly representative of its year and demonstrative of continual progress in research and design.

The first 'North Coast Limited' on the Northern Pacific in 1900 hauled by a Class E5 4-6-0.

At the beginning of the twentieth century a great resurgence of industrial prosperity brought a heavy demand for railroad freight transportation. A trend had already developed toward larger capacity cars, bringing its corollary of increasing train tonnage requiring better roadbeds, heavier rails, stronger bridges, and more powerful locomotives. Reflecting the changes and new requirements in railroad practice, locomotive design kept pace with such progress, often, in fact, anticipating other improvements.

In the early years of the century, most locomotive development was concentrated upon bigger and heavier machines with increased horsepower to handle growing train weights. Some thought, however, was given to improving efficiency, as is evidenced by the several types of compounds. Generally, the accent and concentration on efficiency was to come later as mere size began to reach definite limitations. Larger boilers brought different wheel arrangements; the invention of stokers for the larger fireboxes, superheaters, and the use of oil for fuel in districts where it became plentiful were natural results of necessity and circumstances.

In order to obtain greater steaming capacity which, of course, would be reflected in more power, the first step was to design a wider firebox extending over the frames and located behind the driving wheels. This inevitably led to the use of trailing wheels in order to support such a firebox and thus the Atlantic type (4-4-2) evolved from the American type

The 'Prosperity Special' heading west through the Philadelphia suburbs on the Pennsylvania's Main Line.

8

(4-4-0). In logical sequence, the Prairie type (2-6-2) came from the Mogul, the Mikado (2-8-2) from the Consolidation, the Pacific (4-6-2) from the ten-wheeler, and the Santa Fe (2-10-2) resulted by applying the two-wheeled trailing truck to the Decapod. In the middle 1920's the four-wheeled trailer, usually but not always carrying a booster, was similarly designed to carry the still much larger fireboxes and stokers, thus creating the Berkshire, Texas, Hudson, and Northern types. Meanwhile the four-wheeled lead truck continued to be standard for passenger engines and the two-wheeled type remained standard for freight power except where Mountain or Northern types were designed for such service.

As the larger boilers and over-all weight increased in locomotives, additional pairs of driving wheels were added both for more traction and to better carry and distribute the load on the rails. This load per driving

The Chicago & North Western's '400' leaving Chicago in the late 1930s.

axle has continued to grow with the roadbed and rails necessarily keeping pace in order to carry it. Weights per driving axle were about 43,000 pounds in 1905 while today some steam locomotives have an axle load of nearly 80,000 pounds. With this, horsepower per axle has increased from 300 to 400 in the early 1900's to over 1,500, or for an average locomotive well over 350 per cent. Meanwhile the percentage of weight on the driving wheels has decreased from about 75 per cent to around 55 per cent. Average tractive power has increased 75 per cent.

Many factors contributed largely to improving steam motive power. Outside valve gear such as Walschaerts was first used in 1904 and 1905; other types later applied included Baker, Young, Joy, and Southern. Two most important contributions were the automatic stoker and the superheater, which began to be installed about 1910. Still later came feedwater heaters, boosters, mechanical lubricators, siphons, roller bearings, and many other improvements, all developed to help make the modern steam locomotive the efficient and complex machine it is.

Another important part of the story concerns methods and materials. Improvements in these fields grew with the innovations of locomotive types and appliances, with considerable emphasis on strength in view of increasing weight. Frames, for instance, formerly forged are now largely steel castings, and in the most modern types of engines they are cast integral with cross members and cylinders, forming what is called a "locomotive bed." New types of driving wheel centers have replaced the former spoked wheels. Various leading, trailing, and tender trucks are cast integral rather than being assembled of separate frames and bolsters. Nickel steel is now widely used in boilers, and other alloys are found in other component locomotive parts. Aluminum is sometimes used for cabs and runboards to decrease weight. Welding is done instead of riveting wherever practicable and also plays a very important part in repairs and maintenance. Of course, these developments mentioned give only the barest outline of what research and design have accomplished in locomotive building and maintenance over the past five decades.

In the early 1900's several types of compound locomotives were built in fairly large numbers. Some of these were the Vauclain (4 cylinder), Cole (4 cylinder), Baldwin cross compound (2 cylinder), Schenectady cross compound (2 cylinder), tandem compound (4 cylinder), balanced compound (4 cylinder), and the three-cylinder compound. The object was to effect economy in fuel, but, while the principle still is sound, it never gained too much popularity in rigid frame locomotives, most applications being represented by the Mallets. Of all the railroads operating compounds, the Santa Fe had perhaps the most, a total of 956 various types being listed in their roster.

The principle of articulation in locomotives is not new; it was first used in the "South Carolina" built in 1832 for the Charleston & Hamburg

No. 2102, a streamlined Pacific which in 1939 hauled the 'John Wilkes' on the Lehigh Valley.

Railroad. Another engine of this type was the "Fairlie" of 1864, and in 1876 Anatole Mallet used articulation for his compound. The first combination of these two ideas to be built in this country was the Baltimore & Ohio's Mallet of 1904 (page 42). In this locomotive as in most succeeding ones, a number of Santa Fe articulateds being notable exceptions, the rear main frames are rigid with the boiler and the forward frames connected to these by a pivot joint can swivel from this point and support the front part of the boiler on sliding bearings. Thus an engine will have two short rigid wheelbases with considerable tractive power, less slippage possibility, and better load distribution on the rails. When compounded, steam through the high-pressure cylinders drives the rear set of driving wheels and the exhausted steam from these enters the larger low-pressure cylinders to drive the forward set. When not compounded all four cylinders are generally the same size, almost all articulateds today being of this "single expansion" type. While some are used in passenger service, most are designed for handling the heaviest freight traffic.

11

Tenders, too, have necessarily kept pace with the growth of locomotives. In the 1900's their water capacity averaged about 5,000 gallons but the latest types can carry up to 26,000 gallons. In fuel space they have grown from about a 10-ton capacity to the 46-ton capacity size. In construction they are considerably different from the early types, which were little more than rectangular tanks with extra water capacity either side of the coal space. Improvements began with a "water bottom" under the entire coal space and, more recently, welding the tank sheets instead of riveting has overcome the leakage problem. Cast steel underframes have developed into combined frame and water bottoms. The latest large-capacity tenders have cast tender beds which have pedestals cast integrally for carrying four to six pairs of wheels, a truck being used at the forward end. The trend to these large tenders came as the result of longer locomotive runs; delays formerly caused by coal and water stops are thus largely avoided and high speed schedules can be better maintained.

Through the first half of the twentieth century locomotive building, like other industries, has been affected by wars and depressions. The ac-

The Lehigh Valley's 'Black Diamond' at Ox Bow curve in 1940.

A Baltimore & Ohio Class EM-1 articulated crossing the summit of the Alleghenies with a coal drag.

companying table indicates the decrease in production through the recessions of 1907, 1921, and the early 1930's. Both World Wars brought greater construction of motive power as the need for expedited freight and military equipment movements required. World War I, too, brought a number of standard designs for locomotives as planned by the United States Railroad Administration.

LOCOMOTIVES ORDERED and BUILT SINCE 1900

YEAR	ORDERED			
	STEAM	DIESEL	ELECTRIC	BUILT
1900				2648
1905				4896
1906				6232
1907				6564
1908				1886
1909				2596
1910				4441
1911				3143
1912				4403
1913				4561
1914				1962
1915	1612			1250

YEAR	ORDERED STEAM	DIESEL	ELECTRIC	BUILT
1916	2910			2708
1917	2704			2585
1918	2593			3668
1919	214			2162
1920	1998			2022
1921	239			1185
1922	2600			1303
1923	1944			3505
1924	1413			1810
1925	1055			994
1926	1301			1585
1927	734			1009
1928	603			636
1929	1230			926
1930	382	18	21	972
1931	62	21	91	181
1932	5	7		102
1933	17	25		57
1934	72	37	76	91
1935	30	60	7	184
1936	435	77	24	157
1937	173	145	36	526
1938	36	160	29	272
1939	119	249	32	338
1940	207	492	13	435
1941	293	937	38	1047
1942	363	894	12	936
1943	413	635		1012
1944	74	680	3	1171
1945	148	691	6	935
1946	55	856	8	690
1947	79	2149	1	*
1948	54	2661	2	*
1949	13	1785	10	*

(These figures courtesy Railway Age and Railway Mechanical Engineer.)

Up to 1930, figures include Canadian locomotives. Discrepancies between numbers ordered and built may be accounted for by railroad shop-built equipment not included in orders. Engines ordered not necessarily completed in same year.

The 6318, a Texas type, with a heavy coal train on the Burlington.

An interesting sidelight of the 1921 depression was the "Prosperity Special." In the fall of that year, the Southern Pacific ordered fifty Santa Fe–type locomotives from Baldwin's, which were completed the following spring. To help improve business by means of a tangible demonstration, Mr. Samuel Vauclain, then President of the Baldwin Works, had twenty of these engines shipped across the continent as a single train. Leaving Eddystone on May 26, 1922, this special traveled over the Pennsylvania to East St. Louis, then by the St. Louis–Southwestern to Corsicana, Texas, from where the Southern Pacific took it to Los Angeles. It arrived on July 4, after covering 3,743 miles. The "Prosperity Special" was widely publicized and seen by many thousands on its cross-country trip.

To replace the 41,000 or so steam locomotives now in existence will be a lengthy and costly procedure so, despite the fact that they are no longer being built commercially, they will be seen on our railroads for many years to come. Some new ones will be built by the roads serving the major coal fields. Experiments are continuing with gas turbine power using pulverized coal, but conclusive results are not yet available. Electric power and traction might be expanded—such locomotives by actual comparative tests are ahead of steam and diesel engines on most counts—although increased use of this type of power is not particularly indicated at present. Thus the diesel appears to have a fairly clear field in all three types of service—passenger, freight, and switching. As this book's purpose is more illustrative and historical, no prediction as to future motive power will be attempted. Something, however, will be missing from the American landscape, and the book's real purpose is to pay tribute to a few of the Steel Steeds which were once an important part of the scene.

No. 700 Wabash

CONTENTS

		PAGE
PREFACE		5
INTRODUCTION		7

LIST OF ILLUSTRATIONS

Chicago & North Western Railway
No. 1015   4-4-2   23
Erie Railroad   No. 521   4-4-2   25
Plant System   No. 110   4-6-0   27
St. Louis, Iron Mountain & Southern
Railway   No. 1805   4-8-0   29
New York Central & Hudson River
Railroad   No. 2980   4-4-2   31
St. Louis, Iron Mountain & Southern
Railway   No. 1626   4-6-2   33
Chesapeake & Ohio Railway
No. 147   4-6-2   35
Lake Shore & Michigan Southern
No. 695   2-6-2   37
Atchison, Topeka & Santa Fe
Railway   No. 917   2-10-2   39
Philadelphia & Reading
No. 383   2-6-4 T   41
Baltimore & Ohio Railroad
No. 2400   0-6-6-0   43
Pennsylvania Railroad
No. 1223   4-4-0   45
Northern Pacific Railway
No. 1529   2-8-2   47
Atlantic Coast Line Railroad
No. 139   0-6-0   49
Nashville, Chattanooga & St. Louis
Railway   No. 280   4-6-0   51
Pennsylvania Railroad
No. 1   2-8-0   53
Northern Pacific Railway
No. 2450   2-6-2   55
Chicago, Burlington & Quincy
Railroad   No. 2828   4-6-2   57
Northern Pacific Railway
No. 328   4-6-0   59

New York, New Haven & Hartford
Railroad   No. 1009   4-6-2   61
Chicago, Rock Island & Pacific
Railroad   No. 1799   2-8-0   63
Erie Railroad   No. 2602   0-8-8-0   65
Great Northern Railway
No. 1800   2-6-6-2   67
Reading Company
No. 303   4-4-2   69
Western Pacific Railroad
No. 94   4-6-0   71
Southern Pacific Railroad
No. 4000   2-8-8-2   73
Atchison, Topeka & Santa Fe
Railway   No. 1301   4-4-6-2   75
Pennsylvania Railroad
No. 5075   4-4-2   77
Atchison, Topeka & Santa Fe
Railway   No. 1493   4-4-2   79
Southern Pacific Railroad
No. 4102   4-8-8-2   81
Atchison, Topeka & Santa Fe
Railway   No. 3322   2-6-6-2   83
Seaboard Air Line Railroad
No. 89   4-6-2   85
Chesapeake & Ohio Railway
No. 318   4-8-2   87
Atchison, Topeka & Santa Fe
Railway   No. 3000   2-10-10-2   89
New York Central Railroad
No. 3406   4-6-2   91
Chicago, Rock Island & Pacific
Railroad   No. 2536   2-8-2   93
Chicago, Rock Island & Pacific
Railroad   No. 961   4-6-2   95

Delaware, Lackawanna & Western
  Railroad   No. 1156   4-6-2   97
Pennsylvania Railroad
  No. 1737   4-6-2   99
Erie Railroad   No. 5014
  2-8-8-2   101
St. Louis, Southwestern Railway
  No. 412   2-6-0   103
Reading Company
  No. 110   4-4-4   105
Minneapolis & St. Louis Railway
  No. 615   2-8-2   107
Reading Company
  No. 1817   2-8-8-2   109
Chesapeake & Ohio Railway
  No. 137   4-8-2   111
Chicago & Eastern Illinois Railroad
  No. 1925   2-8-2   113
Pennsylvania Railroad
  No. 7246   2-10-2   115
Louisville & Nashville Railroad
  No. 1462   2-8-2   117
Pennsylvania Railroad
  No. 3700   2-8-8-0   119
Illinois Central Railroad
  No. 2814   2-10-2   121
Atchison, Topeka & Santa Fe
  Railway   No. 4000   2-8-2   123
Louisville & Nashville Railroad
  No. 255   4-6-2   125
Pennsylvania Railroad
  No. 6813   4-8-2   127
Missouri Pacific Railroad
  No. 1430   2-8-2   129
Illinois Central Railroad
  No. 1986   2-8-2   131
Northern Pacific Railway
  No. 1844   2-8-2   133
Lehigh Valley Railroad
  No. 2092   4-6-2   135
Maine Central Railroad
  No. 469   4-6-2   137
Lima Locomotive Works
  No. 1   2-8-4   139

Texas & Pacific Railway
  No. 600   2-10-4   141
Canadian National Railways
  No. 6038   4-8-2   143
Chesapeake & Ohio Railway
  No. 1572   2-8-8-2   145
Union Pacific Railroad
  No. 9085   4-12-2   147
Baldwin Locomotive Works
  No. 60,000   4-10-2   149
New York Central Railroad
  No. 5297   4-6-4   151
Richmond, Fredericksburg &
  Potomac Railroad
  No. 325   4-6-2   153
Illinois Central Railroad
  No. 3540   0-8-0   155
Denver & Rio Grande Western
  Railroad   No. 3603   2-8-8-2   157
Chicago, Burlington & Quincy
  Railroad   No. 6318   2-10-4   159
Boston & Albany Railroad
  No. 400   4-6-6 T   161
Texas & Pacific Railway
  No. 909   4-8-2   163
Baltimore & Ohio Railroad
  No. 5320   4-6-2   165
Minneapolis, St. Paul & Saulte Ste.
  Marie Railroad   No. 4018
  4-8-2   167
Great Northern Railway
  No. 2552   4-8-4   169
Southern Railway
  No. 1407   4-6-2   171
Delaware & Hudson Railroad
  No. 652   4-6-2   173
Chicago, Indianapolis & Louisville
  Railway   No. 573   2-8-2   175
Southern Railway
  No. 4052   2-8-8-2   177
Timken Roller Bearing Company
  No. 1111   4-8-4   179
Chicago, Milwaukee, St. Paul
  & Pacific Railroad   No. 6402   181

Northern Pacific Railway
    No. 5002   2-8-8-4   183
Western Pacific Railroad
    No. 254   2-8-8-2   185
Wabash Railroad
    No. 2921   4-8-4   187
Lehigh Valley Railroad
    No. 5103   4-8-4   189
Pittsburgh & West Virginia
    Railway   No. 1101   2-6-6-4   191
Chicago, Milwaukee, St. Paul &
    Pacific Railroad   No. 3   4-4-2   193
Union Railroad   No. 303   0-10-2   195
Norfolk & Western Railway
    No. 1212   2-6-6-4   197
New York, New Haven & Hartford
    Railroad   No. 1400   4-6-4   199
Baltimore & Ohio Railroad
    No. 5600   4-8-4   201
Kansas City Southern Lines
    No. 900   2-10-4   203
Southern Pacific Railroad
    No. 4439   4-8-4   205
Richmond, Fredericksburg &
    Potomac Railroad
    No. 553   4-8-4   207
Denver & Rio Grande Western
    Railroad   No. 1801   4-8-4   209
Canadian Pacific Railway
    No. 2850   4-6-4   211
Minneapolis, St. Paul & Saulte
    Ste. Marie Railroad
    No. 5000   4-8-4   213
Pennsylvania Railroad
    No. 6100   6-4-4-6   215
Atchison, Topeka & Santa Fe
    Railway   No. 5004   2-10-4   217
Detroit, Toledo & Ironton
    Railroad   No. 704   2-8-4   219
Union Pacific Railroad
    No. 4000   4-8-8-4   221
Norfolk & Western Railway
    No. 600   4-8-4   223

Chesapeake & Ohio Railway
    No. 1625   2-6-6-6   225
Pennsylvania Railroad
    No. 6474   2-10-4   227
St. Louis, Southwestern Railway
    No. 815   4-8-4   229
Louisville & Nashville Railroad
    No. 1960   2-8-4   231
Northern Pacific Railway
    No. 5139   4-6-6-4   233
Central of Georgia Railway
    No. 455   4-8-4   235
Pennsylvania Railroad
    No. 6200   6-8-6   237
Pennsylvania Railroad
    No. 6184   4-4-6-4   239
Baltimore & Ohio Railroad
    No. 7600   2-8-8-4   241
Western Maryland Railway
    No. 6   4-4-4   Shay-geared   243
Reading Company
    No. 2100   4-8-4   245
Pennsylvania Railroad
    No. 5505   4-4-4-4   247
New York Central Railroad
    No. 6001   4-8-4   249
Chesapeake & Ohio Railway
    No. 500   4-8-8-4   Turbo-Electric 251
Norfolk & Western Railway
    No. 2156   2-8-8-2   253
New York, Chicago & St. Louis
    Railroad   No. 776   2-8-4   255

First, the shrill whistle, then the distant roar,
The ascending cloud of steam, the gleaming brass,
The mighty moving arm; and on amain
The mass comes thundering, like an avalanche o'er,
The quaking earth; a thousand faces pass—
A moment, and are gone, like whirlwind sprites,
Scarce seen; so much the roaring speed benights
All sense and recognition for a while;
A little space, a minute, and a mile.
Then look again, how swiftly it journeys on;
Away, away, along the horizon
Like drifted cloud, to its determined place;
Power, speed, and distance, melting into space.

(from an unidentified verse
of over one hundred years ago)

1900

Chicago & North Western Railway   NO. 1015   4-4-2

THE ATLANTIC TYPE was so named for its first being built for the Atlantic Coast Line in 1895. This representative Schenectady-built engine at the turn of the century is an almost classic example of simplicity and cleanness in design. It saw service hauling such trains as the Overland Limited.

Builder—American Locomotive Co.

Cylinders—20″ x 26″

Weight, light—202,800 lb.

Steam Pressure—200 lb.

Fuel—8 tons

Water—5,200 gal.

Dia. Drivers—81″

Tractive Effort—22,100 lb.

R.R. Class—D

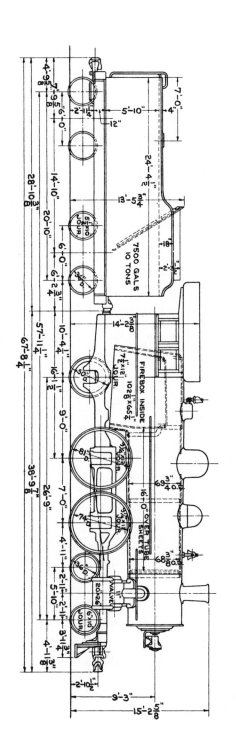

Erie Railroad
NO. 521   4-4-2

ORIGINALLY a Vauclain compound, this Atlantic was rebuilt into a simple type by 1905. When first delivered this class was used in through-line passenger service although not over more than one division. The three photos show the evolution of this type from compound through 1905 rebuilding to latest appearance in 1921.

Builder—Baldwin Locomotive Works

Cylinders—18″ x 26″

Weight, light—172,970 lb.

Steam Pressure—200 lb.

Fuel—12 tons

Water—6,000 gal.

Dia. Drivers—76″

Tractive Effort—18,800 lb.

R.R. Class—E1

Plant System

NO. 110   4-6-0

No. 110 serves to illustrate her somewhat more famous sister, the 111, which set an unofficial speed record of 120 miles per hour in 1901. In March of that year, the Plant System and the Seaboard bid on a new contract for faster mail between Washington and the West Indies. Eight cars of mail from Washington were divided between the two roads at Savannah, and the first to get its four into Jacksonville was to get the contract.

The Plant System ran the four cars as a special, starting with engine No. 107 which reached Fleming where it was delayed with a hot driving box. Here the 111 took over, leaving an hour late. From Jesup to Jacksonville via Waycross—115.9 miles—the trip was made in 90 minutes or at 77.3 miles per hour, while between Screven and Satilla the time was 2 minutes and 30 seconds or at a speed of 120 miles per hour.

The Plant System was acquired by the Atlantic Coast Line in 1902 and the 111 was renumbered 210. It was dismantled in 1942.

Builder—Rhode Island Locomotive Works (Alco)

Cylinders—19" x 28"

Weight, total—252,900 lb.

Steam Pressure—180 lb.

Fuel—9½ tons

Water—5,000 gal.

Tractive Effort—21,240 lb.

R.R. Class—K9

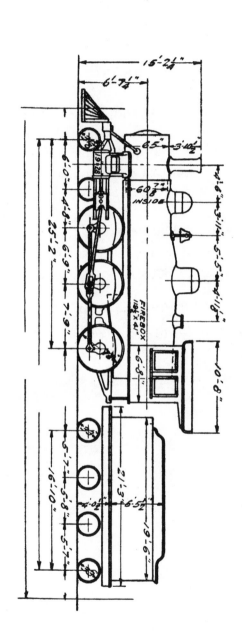

1901

St. Louis, Iron Mountain & Southern Railway

NO. 1805   4-8-0

BUILT AT the Brooks Works at Dunkirk, New York, and designed for freight service, the engines of this class were used over the Mineral Point and Gads Hill grades between De Soto and Piedmont, Missouri. This wheel arrangement never attained very much popularity, Consolidations (2-8-0) being much more generally used in freight traffic.

Builder—American Locomotive Co.

Cylinders—21″ x 32″

Weight, engine—215,150 lb.

Steam Pressure—190 lb.

Fuel—9 coal burners
6 oil burners

Dia. Drivers—55″

Tractive Effort—41,440 lb.

Eng. Nos.—1803 to 1817

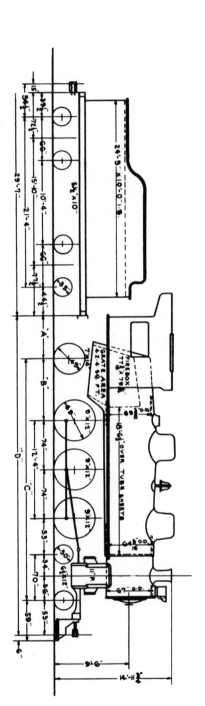

WRONG DIAGRAM 4-6-2

1902

New York Central &

Hudson River Railroad   NO. 2980   4-4-2

THIS LOCOMOTIVE is representative of the first Atlantics used on the New York Central System. It was found so satisfactory in design that no important changes were necessary for five years, during which time a large number were built for the Central. They were used in fast passenger service.

Builder—American Locomotive Co.

Cylinders—21″ x 26″

Weight, total—286,500 lb.

Steam Pressure—200 lb.

Fuel—10 tons

Water—5,000 gal.

Dia. Drivers—79″

Tractive Effort—24,700 lb.

R.R. Class—I10

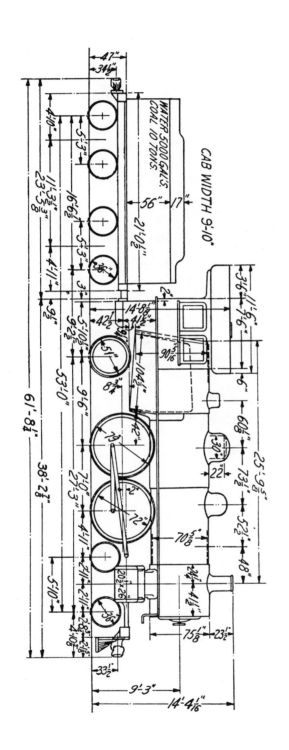

1902

St. Louis, Iron Mountain & Southern Railway

NO. 1626   4-6-2

THE FIRST Pacifics used in this country were these locomotives; in fact, according to most sources, the type was named for their having been built for the Missouri Pacific, although the Baldwin-built machines exported earlier are also credited for naming this wheel arrangement. The St. L., I.M. & S., which was incorporated into the Mo. Pac., used them in passenger service and some were oil burners. Their original numbers were 6501 to 6516.

Builder—American Locomotive Co.

Cylinders—20" x 26"

Weight, engine—193,000 lb.

Steam Pressure—200 lb.

Fuel—10 tons

Water—5,000 gal.

Dia. Drivers—69"

Tractive Effort—26,835 lb.

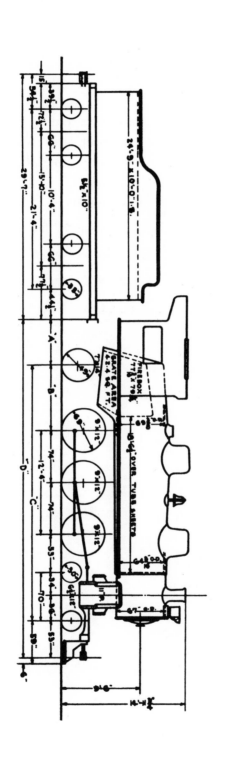

1902

Chesapeake & Ohio Railway

NO. 147   4-6-2

THIS WAS the second Pacific type built for domestic use, also being turned out by the Schenectady Works. It was rebuilt later with Walschaerts valve gear, stoker, and larger tender, and was renumbered 430.

Builder—American Locomotive Co.

Cylinders—22″ x 28″

Weight, light—309,000 lb.

Steam Pressure—200 lb.

Fuel—9 tons

Water—6,000 gal.

Dia. Drivers—72″

Tractive Effort—32,000 lb.

R.R. Class—F15

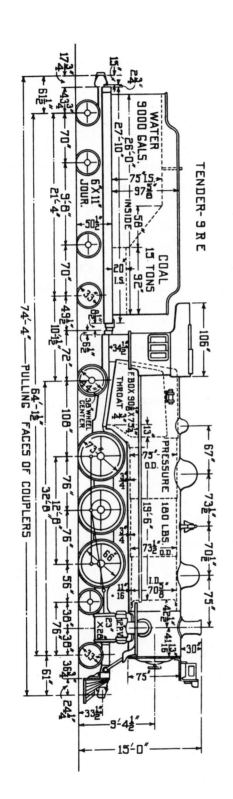

1903

Lake Shore & Michigan Southern   NO. 695   2-6-2

THE PRAIRIE type was the logical development from the 2-6-0 or Mogul as a result of larger boiler capacity and greater tractive power requirements. It was not, however, built in as large numbers as Atlantics, which were developed simultaneously, these proving better at high speed with their four-wheel leading trucks. The engine illustrated is an example of Prairies at the peak of their design. In fact, if the term "graceful" can be applied to a locomotive, this machine particularly deserves it. The 695 was used in fast passenger service and the small lettering on the cab panel advertised the "Universal Exposition, Saint Louis 1904."

Builder—American Locomotive Co.

Cylinders—20½″ x 28″

Weight, total—320,000 lb.

Steam Pressure—200 lb.

Fuel—13 tons

Water—6,000 gal.

Tractive Effort—25,000 lb.

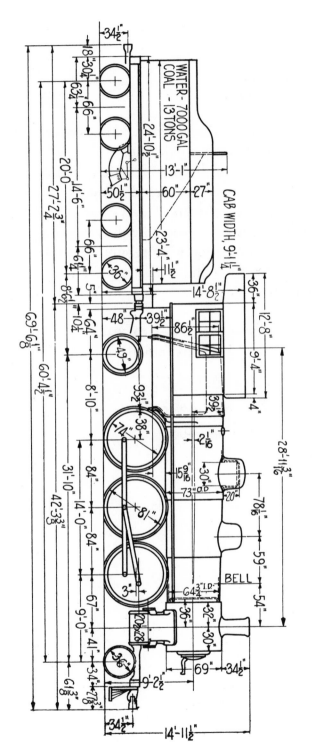

1903

Atchison, Topeka & Santa Fe Railway   NO. 917   2-10-2

THESE WERE the first engines of their wheel arrangement and so gave the name to the type—Santa Fe. They were tandem compounds which had a pair of high-pressure cylinders placed ahead of the low-pressure cylinders located in the usual position. A common piston rod passed through both and the resulting thrust was quite even to the drivers. Thirty-four of this type were delivered to the road in 1903 and fifty-two more the following year, all being used in freight service. Later they were rebuilt as simple engines with 28″ x 32″ cylinders with 200-pound steam pressure and a rated tractive effort of 74,800 pounds.

Builder—Baldwin Locomotive Works

Cylinders—19″ and 32″ x 32″

Weight, light—287,240 lb.

Steam Pressure—225 lb.

Fuel—Nos. 900–939 coal burners; others, oil

Dia. Drivers—57″

Tractive Effort—62,800 lb.

R.R. Class—900

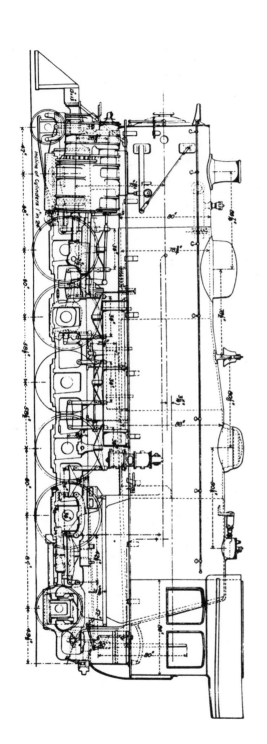

1903

Philadelphia & Reading

NO. 383   2-6-4 T

TEN OF THESE engines known as double-end tank locomotives were used in suburban service in Philadelphia between Reading Terminal and Chestnut Hill. The short runs and impossibility of turning tender engines at the suburban terminus were responsible for the design, and this type was used until electrification of this area in 1931.

Builder—Baldwin Locomotive Works

Cylinders—20″ x 24″

Weight—201,700 lb.

Steam Pressure—200 lb.

Dia. Drivers—61½″

Tractive Effort—26,540 lb.

R.R. Class—Q1b

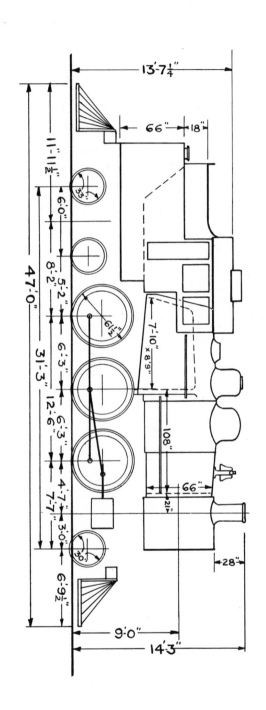

1904

Baltimore & Ohio Railroad   NO. 2400   0-6-6-0

THIS WAS the first Mallet type to be built in the United States, although its forerunner named for its designer appeared in France in 1875. Designed by James E. Muhlfeld of the B. & O. and Carl J. Mellin of the American Locomotive Co., it was completed in time to be exhibited at the St. Louis Exhibition from which it went into service handling freight over the road's heavy western Pennsylvania grades. Not only did it more than exceed expectations in every respect, thus vindicating a number of new features in design, but "Old Maud" inaugurated a trend to such power.

Builder—American Locomotive Co.

Cylinders—20" and 32" x 32"

Weight, total—334,500 lb.

Steam Pressure—235 lb.

Fuel—15 tons

Water—7,000 gal.

Dia. Drivers—56"

Tractive Effort—71,500 lb.

R.R. Class—DD1

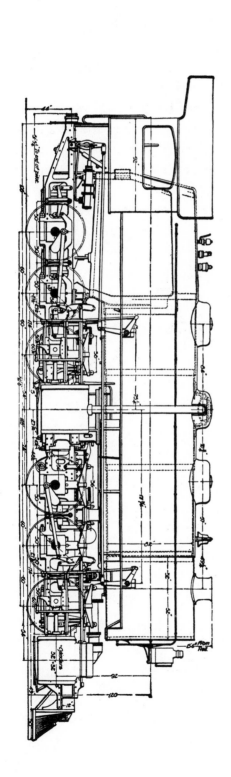

1905

Pennsylvania Railroad

NO. 1223   4-4-0

THE D16 Class of the P.R.R. represents the acme of American-type development on the System and the last of their kind. The class includes a number of variations from D16 through a,b,c,d, to D16sb, the 1223 exemplifying the ultimate in design. Before the advent of the Atlantics, these 4-4-0's pulled the new Pennsylvania Special in 1902 on a twenty-hour schedule between New York and Chicago making an excellent on-time record. The 1223 is being preserved, although some of the more modern fittings have altered its original appearance slightly.

Builder—Juniata Shops

Cylinders—20½″ x 26″

Weight, engine—141,000 lb.

Steam Pressure—175 lb.

Fuel—13 tons, 5,600 gal.

Dia. Drivers—68″

Tractive Effort—23,902 lb.

R.R. Class—D16sb

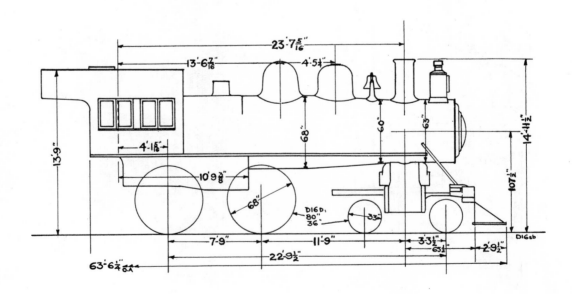

1905

Northern Pacific Railway NO. 1529   2-8-2

MIKADOS WERE designed for and generally used in freight service, although this photo shows such an engine at Gardiner, Montana, at the northern entrance to Yellowstone Park, September, 1940. No. 1529 was one of one hundred and sixty Class W engines built by the Brooks Works from 1904 to 1907, eighty-seven of which are still in service. It was one of the first on the N.P. to be converted from coal to oil, this being done particularly because of the tourist trade, for which open-air observations were used.

Builder—American Locomotive Co.

Cylinders—24″ x 30″

Weight—263,500 lb.

Steam Pressure—200 lb.

Fuel—12 tons (orig.)
        3,449 gal. oil

Water—8,000 gal.

Dia. Drivers—63″

Tractive Effort—46,600 lb.

R.R. Class—W

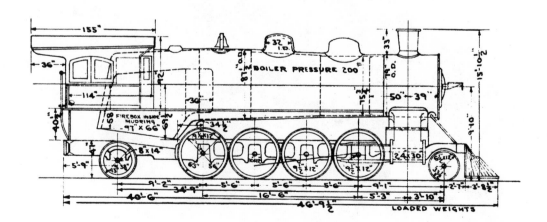

1905

Atlantic Coast Line Railroad   NO. 139   0-6-0

THIS SWITCHER was built for the Wilmington & Weldon Railroad, a part of the A.C.L. It represents a typical switching engine of the early 1900's and was one of a fleet of such locomotives numbered from 126 to 185. Some were Baldwin-built and others were supplied by American.

Builder—Richmond Works (Alco)

Cylinders—19″ x 24″

Weight—163,365 lb.

Steam Pressure—180 lb.

Fuel—7 tons

Water—2,500 gal.

Dia. Drivers—51″

Tractive Effort—26,510 lb.

R.R. Class—E4

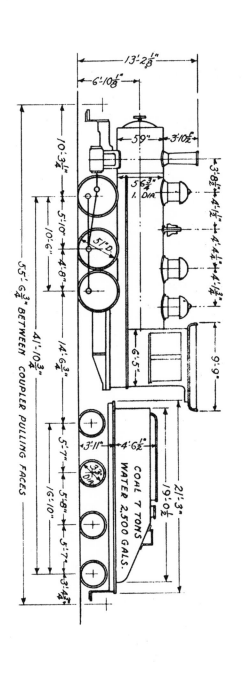

1905

Nashville, Chattanooga & St. Louis Railway

NO. 280   4-6-0

THIS TEN-WHEELER was modified since the early photo was taken—piston valve cylinders, Walschaerts valve gear, and power reverse are among the improvements. It was a heavy passenger engine for its day, and records indicate that it is still in service.

Builder—Baldwin Locomotive Works

Cylinders—22″ x 26″

Weight, total—302,900 lb.

Steam Pressure—200 lb.

Fuel—10½ tons

Water—6,000 gal.

Dia. Drivers—66″

Tractive Effort—32,400 lb.

R.R. Class—68A32

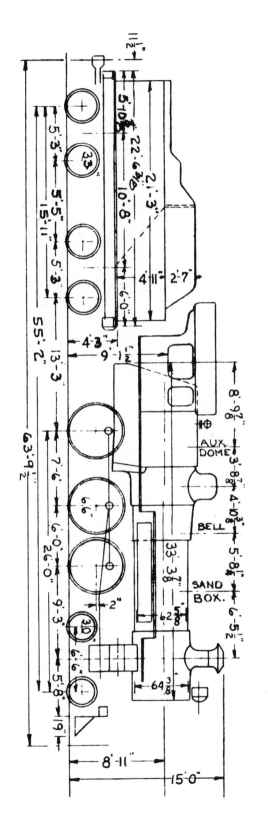

1905

Pennsylvania Railroad

NO. 1   2-8-0

CONSOLIDATIONS such as this were built in large numbers for heavy freight service. Walschaerts valve gear was first applied to ten such engines (H6b) built by Baldwin's and the results were so satisfactory that it was installed on all others then under construction. Between October 10 and November 22, 1905, the Baldwin Works completed one hundred and sixty Class H6b engines and through 1907 delivered four hundred and twenty-three. The "s" in the railroad classification denotes it was superheated.

Builder—Baldwin Locomotive
   Works

Cylinders—22″ x 28″

Weight, engine—204,800 lb.

Steam Pressure—205 lb.

Fuel—14 tons

Water—7,200 gal.

Dia. Drivers—56″

Tractive Effort—42,170 lb.

R.R. Class—H6sb

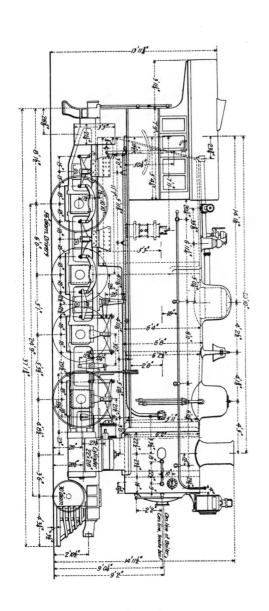

1906

Northern Pacific Railway

NO. 2450   2-6-2

THIS IS ONE of one hundred and fifty Prairie-type locomotives built for the N.P. by the Brooks Works during 1906 and 1907. Eighteen are still on the roster of motive power and fourteen are still in service. The photo was made in June, 1947, at St. Paul. As they were too light for mountain service, nearly all were assigned to the St. Paul–Duluth and Mandan territory and a few were used on the Idaho Division. All are used for switching.

Builder—American Locomotive Co.

Cylinders—21½″ x 28″

Weight, engine—208,500 lb.

Steam Pressure—200 lb.

Fuel—10¹⁄₁₀ tons

Water—7,000 gal.

Dia. Drivers—63″

Tractive Effort—35,000 lb.

R.R. Class—T1

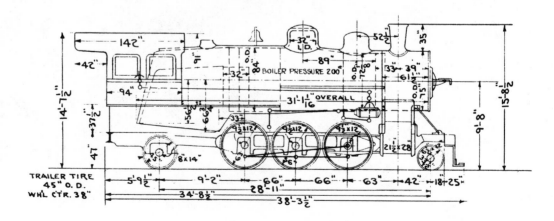

Chicago, Burlington & Quincy Railroad

NO. 2828   4-6-2

THIS PACIFIC is considered by the road's Motive Power Department to be one of the milestones among their twentieth-century locomotives. It was one of seventy built from 1906 to 1909 and the photo shows its original appearance. All this class were rebuilt through the twenties and most are still on the road's roster, although evidently not for long as dieselization progresses.

Builder—Baldwin Locomotive Works and American Locomotive Co.

Cylinders—23″ x 28″

Weight, total—425,790 lb.

Steam Pressure—200 lb.

Fuel—13 tons

Water—9,000 gal.

Dia. Drivers—74″

Tractive Effort—34,000 lb.

R.R. Class—S1a

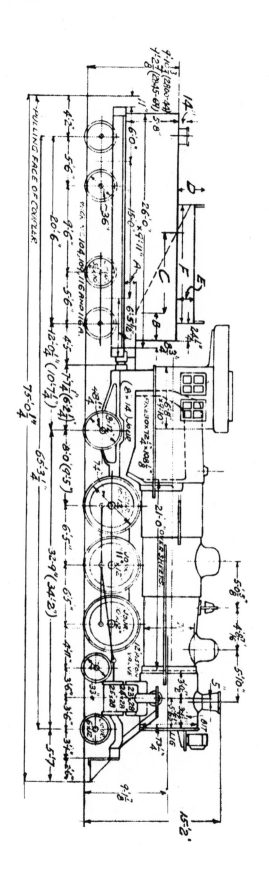

1907

Northern Pacific Railway

NO. 328   4-6-0

THIS WAS one of ten Rogers-built ten-wheelers originally ordered for export but acquired by the N.P. when the original purchasers refused acceptance. Being too light and top heavy for main-line service, they were used in branch-line work. The photo was made at Wyoming, Minnesota, in September, 1946, when the 328 was assigned to the now-abandoned Taylors Falls Branch. It is the only one of its class still in existence.

Builder—American Locomotive Co.

Cylinders—19″ x 26″

Weight, engine—153,000 lb.

Steam Pressure—190 lb.

Fuel—8 tons

Water—5,000 gal.

Dia. Drivers—57″

Tractive Effort—26,600 lb.

R.R. Class—S10

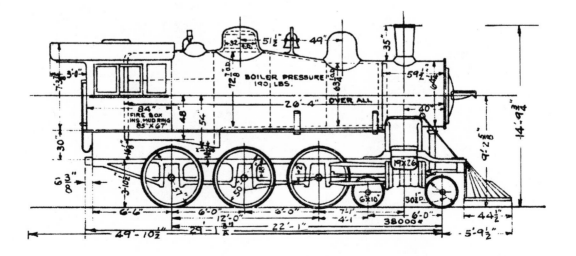

1907

New York, New Haven & Hartford Railroad

NO. 1009   4-6-2

THE 1009 WAS one of a fleet of twenty Pacifics of this class which pulled the Merchants, the Bay State, and the Knickerbocker Limiteds some forty years ago. These were Baldwin-built while another eight were Alco machines, two more of the latter being added to the roster in 1910. In 1917 piston valve cylinders replaced the slide valve type and superheated steam used. They were last operated in local service out of Boston and at the present time three are still on call.

Builder—Baldwin (Nos. 1009–1029)
    Alco (1000–1008, 1030, 1031)
Cylinders—22″ x 28″
Weight, engine—227,000 lb.
Steam Pressure—200 lb.

Fuel—14 tons
Water—6,000 gal.
Dia. Drivers—73″
Tractive Effort—31,550 lb.
R.R. Class—I1

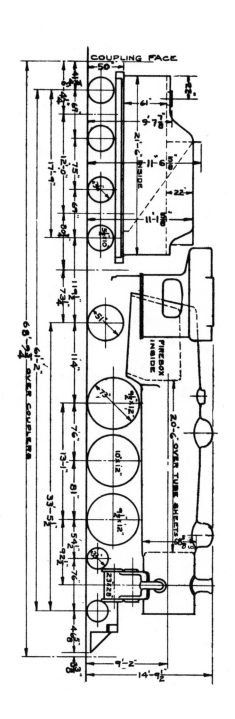

1907

Chicago, Rock Island & Pacific Railroad

NO. 1799   2-8-0

THIS CONSOLIDATION is representative of the R.I., but from records available, although so lettered, it was not accepted by the road because it was too heavy on the drivers. Instead, the 2200 was delivered, this being according to specifications although otherwise essentially the same. It was subsequently modified in 1921 but retained the same wheel arrangement and was renumbered 1784.

Builder—Baldwin Locomotive Works

Cylinders—25½″ x 32″

Weight, total—400,870 lb.

Steam Pressure—185 lb.

Fuel—15 tons

Water—9,000 gal.

Dia. Drivers—63″

Tractive Effort—49,130 lb.

R.R. Class—60, Road Class C49

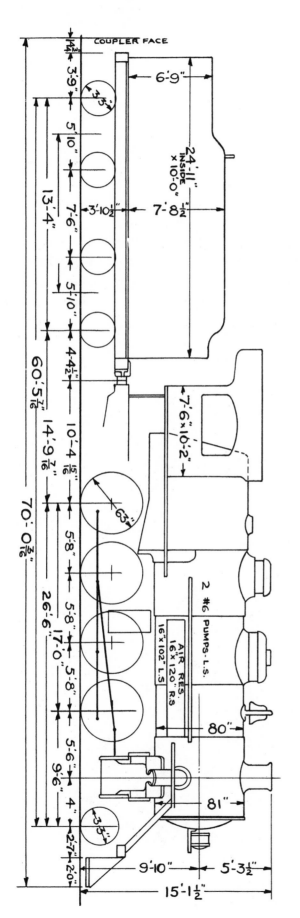

COUPLER FACE

24'-11" INSIDE × 10'-0"

7'-6"×10'-2"

2 #6 PUMPS- L.S.

AIR RES.
16'×120" R.S
16"×102" L.S

ROCK ISLAND

1799

1799

1907

Erie Railroad

NO. 2602   0-8-8-0

THERE WERE three of these first Mallets on the Erie, and they are particularly interesting as being the only "camelback" engines of such wheel arrangement ever built. They were primarily used in pushing service and especially on the heavy grades of the Delaware and Susquehanna Divisions. When rebuilt in 1921 with a pair of leading and trailing wheels, the cab was moved back over the firebox. The original designation was "Angus" type.

Builder—American Locomotive Co.

Cylinders—25″ x 28″, 39″ x 28″

Weight, light—424,000 lb.

Steam Pressure—215 lb.

Fuel—16 tons

Water—8,500 gal.

Dia. Drivers—51″

Tractive Effort—94,070 lb.

R.R. Class—L1

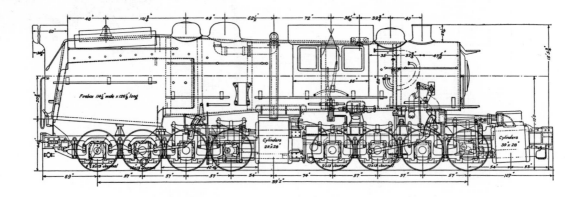

1908

Great Northern Railway

NO. 1800   2-6-6-2

ANOTHER VERY early Mallet was this engine, one of forty-five built through 1907 and 1908. Designed for heavy freight service in the Rockies and Cascade Mountains, they were coal burners. All were dismantled between 1922 and 1925 and Class O5 Mikados built from the parts at various shops on the System.

Builder—Baldwin Locomotive Works

Cylinders—20″ x 30″, 31″ x 30″

Weight, total—451,000 lb.

Steam Pressure—200 lb.

Fuel—16 tons

Water—8,000 gal.

Tractive Effort—54,520 lb.

R.R. Class—L2

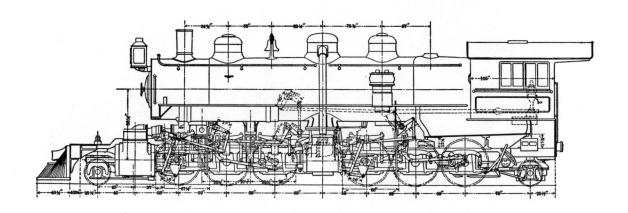

1909

Reading Company

THE 303 WAS one of three three-cylinder locomotives built at the Reading Shops. It was designed by the company's chief draftsman, Edward O. Elliott, and besides being notable for the extra cylinder arrangement, it was the first engine on the Reading to have Walschaerts valve gear. The 300 was very similar but the 344 rebuilt from a P5a in 1912 varied in a number of details. The three were used in high-speed passenger service on the New York–Philadelphia and the Camden–Atlantic City runs. All were rebuilt as simple engines in 1916 and 1917.

Builder—Reading Shops

Cylinders—18½″ x 24″

Weight, total—226,700 lb.

Steam Pressure—225 lb.

Dia. Drivers—80″

Tractive Effort—29,454 lb.

R.R. Class—Q1b

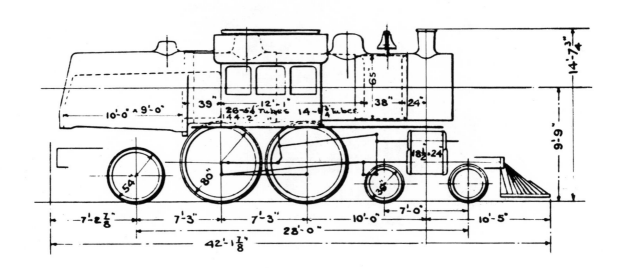

1909

Western Pacific Railroad

NO. 94   4-6-0

No. 94 WAS the first engine to pull a passenger train through the Feather River Canyon. It was one of twenty ten-wheelers which were numbered 86 to 106. It has been restored to its original appearance since the photo was taken; this includes a higher old-style headlight, striping on domes, and other characteristics of the period.

Builder—American Locomotive Co.

Cylinders—21" x 26"

Weight, total—316,800 lb.

Steam Pressure—200 lb.

Fuel—3,019 gal. oil

Water—7,000 gal.

Dia. Drivers—67"

Tractive Effort—29,100 lb.

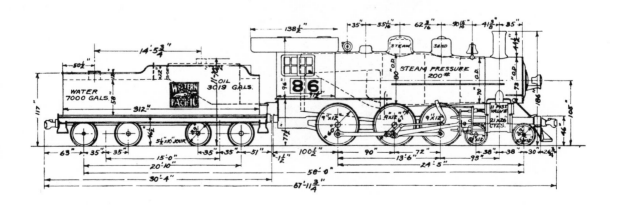

1909

Southern Pacific Railroad

NO. 4000   2-8-8-2

THIS WAS one of the first two Mallet compounds built for the Southern Pacific for use over the Sierras. From Roseville to Summit the vertical rise is 6,623 feet in 89 miles or a 2.65 per cent ruling grade, and these engines were designed and intended to be used on this part of the S.P. But although their performance was up to expectations, their use through the snowsheds led to the first "cab ahead" type, and they were assigned elsewhere on the system (see p. 81).

Builder—Baldwin Locomotive
    Works

Steam Pressure—210 lb.

Dia. Drivers—57"

R.R. Class—MC

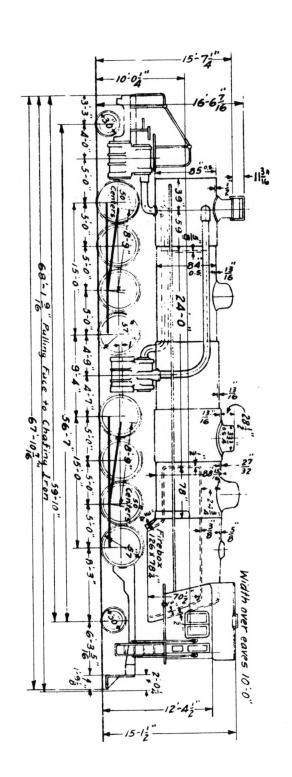

1909

Atchison, Topeka & Santa Fe Railway   NO. 1301   4-4-6-2

THIS AND her sister engine, the 1300, are particularly interesting for several reasons. They were the first Mallets to have a four-wheel leading truck, they had the largest driving wheels ever applied to articulated engines, they were the largest and most powerful passenger locomotives when built, and they were the first to have this wheel arrangement. Six years after they first went into service they were rebuilt into Pacifics.

Builder—Baldwin Locomotive
　Works

Cylinders—28″ and 38″ x 28″

Weight, total—376,850 lb.

Steam Pressure—200 lb.

Dia. Drivers—73″

Tractive Effort—53,700 lb.

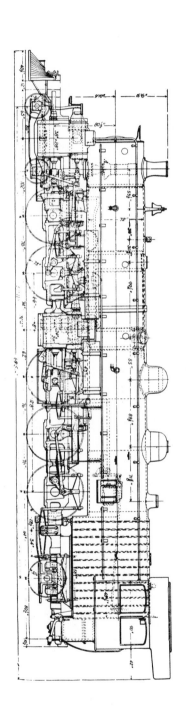

1910

Pennsylvania Railroad NO. 5075 4-4-2

THIS WAS the first of the famous E6 Class of Atlantics, although following ones were superheated. It underwent a series of tests at the Altoona testing plant and was tried in passenger service pulling up to fifteen cars at 58.05 miles an hour. One of its runs was from Altoona to Philadelphia, 235 miles, which it made at 67.4 miles per hour (deducting for a three-minute stop at Harrisburg). Running between Fort Wayne and Valparaiso, Indiana, it was compared with other power, was found to have equal drawbar pull to the K2 Pacific at 40 miles per hour, and could better this at higher speed. The 5075 was superheated and renumbered 1067 in 1912; it was followed by large numbers of similar engines (E6s) which handled most of the Pennsylvania's high-speed traffic until the K4 Pacific was developed.

Builder—Juniata Shops
Cylinders—22″ x 26″
Weight, total—231,500 lb.
Steam Pressure—205 lb.

Fuel—15⅝ tons
Water—7,150 gal.
Dia. Drivers—80″
Tractive Effort—27,410 lb.
R.R. Class—E6

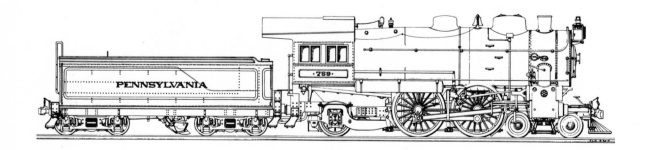

1910

Atchison, Topeka & Santa Fe Railway   NO. 1493   4-4-2

"Unusual" hardly describes the twenty-three peculiar-looking Atlantics of this class—in fact, they were called "Bull Moosers" because of their ungainly appearance. They had Jacobs-Shupert fireboxes and smokebox reheaters and were four-cylinder balanced compounds. The form of Walschaerts valve gear was also unusual. Nine of the lot were scrapped and the others were rebuilt through the twenties into simple locomotives. In the process, their boilers were shortened, the resulting engines being much more conventional in appearance.

Builder—Baldwin Locomotive Works

Cylinders—15" and 25" x 26"

Weight, total—231,675 lb.

Steam Pressure—220 lb.

Dia. Drivers—73"

Tractive Effort—24,000 lb.

R.R. Class—1480

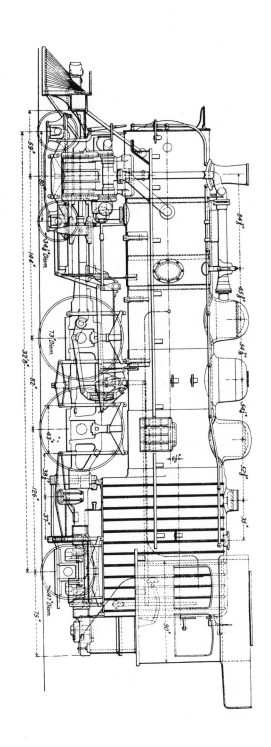

1910

Southern Pacific Railroad

NO. 4102   4-8-8-2

WHILE THIS is not the original "cab-ahead" engine, it was one of the earlier ones. The principal reason for this cab location was the 38-mile series of snowsheds between Truckee and Blue Canyon built to keep the line open in winter when drifts of fifty to two hundred feet deep piled up in the passes. When the 4000 and 4001 were operated through these snowsheds (see p. 73), their crews were all too frequently overcome by the gases. The new design was developed to overcome this objection as well as to increase visibility. Fuel oil was piped the length of the engine at five pounds pressure from the tender, and locomotive and tender positions were reversed, thus creating this cab-ahead type. Fifteen engines constituted the original order and these were compounds. In recent years the S.P. had a fleet of over two hundred such power, although all were single expansion locomotives, conversions of the older engines having been started in 1927.

FIRST CAB-AHEAD TYPE—AC1

Builder—Baldwin Locomotive Works

Cylinders—22″ x 30″ (rebuilt simple)

Weight, engine—481,200 lb.

Steam Pressure—210 lb.

Fuel—3,817 gal. oil

Water—12,000 gal.

Dia. Drivers—57″

Tractive Effort—90,940 lb.

LOCOMOTIVE ILLUSTRATED—AC4

Builder—Baldwin Locomotive Works

Cylinders—24″ x 32″ (simple)

Weight, engine—614,000 lb.

Steam pressure—235 lb.

Fuel—4,889 gal. oil

Water—16,152 gal.

Dia. Drivers—63″

Tractive Effort—116,900 lb.

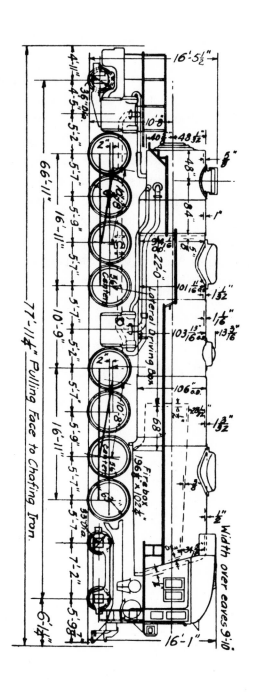

1911

Atchison, Topeka & Santa Fe Railway NO. 3322   2-6-6-2

THIS WAS another very unusual type of Mallet in that it had a hinged boiler. Fifty rings of high carbon steel the diameter of the boiler shell and ten inches wide were riveted together alternatively at their inner and outer edges to form a metal bellows which joined the two boiler sections. These were each bolted to an engine frame and only one flexible steam pipe, that connecting to the high-pressure cylinders, was required. Trouble was experienced when cinders got into the folds of the bellows causing them to burst on curves. Other types of flexible boiler arrangements were also experimented with on some six succeeding engines, but none were entirely satisfactory. Although other Mallets were built later in the Santa Fe Shops, these were the last purchased by the railroad.

Builder—Baldwin Locomotive
   Works
Cylinders—24″ and 38″ x 28″
Weight, total—381,800 lb.
Steam Pressure—220 lb.

Dia. Drivers—69″
Tractive Effort—62,400 lb.
R.R. Class—3300

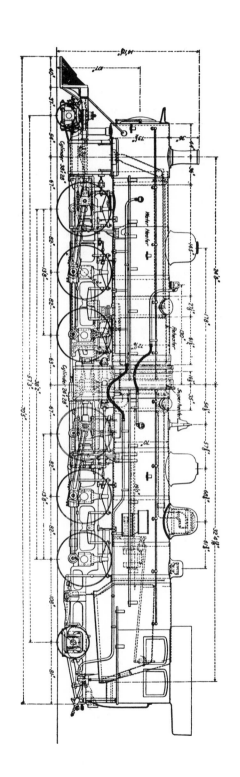

1911

Seaboard Air Line Railroad

NO. 89   4-6-2

No. 89 WAS one of a group of light Pacifics built from 1911 to 1913 and used to handle principal passenger trains on the S.A.L. Fifty more Pacifics, very similar but somewhat heavier and with smaller drivers, were also built in this period for freight service.

Builder—Baldwin Locomotive
Works (5)
American Locomotive Co.
(15)

Cylinders—23″ x 28″

Weight, total—366,040 lb.

Steam Pressure—195 lb.

Fuel—14 tons

Water—8,000 gal.

Dia. Drivers—72″

Tractive Effort—34,100 lb.

R.R. Class—P (Nos. 85 to 104)

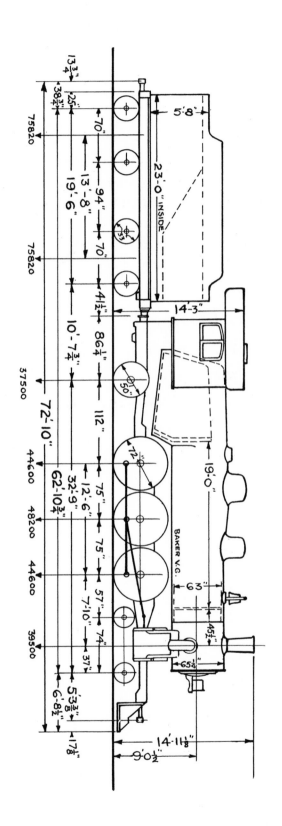

1911

Chesapeake & Ohio Railway   NO. 318   4-8-2

HERE IS one of the first two locomotives having another new wheel arrangement—the Mountain type, so named for its having been designed to handle 600 to 700-ton passenger trains over 1 in 60 and 1 in 70 grades of the Clifton Forge Division in the Alleghenies. Disregarding articulated types, they were claimed to be the world's most powerful passenger locomotives when built. Two were delivered in 1911 and one the following year, these later being numbered 540, 541, and 542.

Builder—American Locomotive Co. (Richmond Works)

Cylinders—29″ x 28″

Weight, total—499,500 (original)

Steam Pressure—180 lb.

Fuel—15 tons

Water—9,000 gal. (original)

Dia. Drivers—62″

Tractive Effort—58,000 lb.

R.R. Class (present)—J1

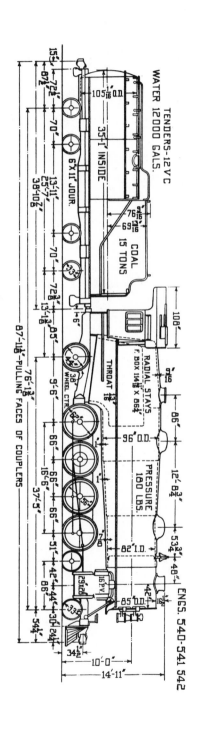

TENDERS-12 V C
WATER 12000 GALS.

105 5/16 O.D.

35'-1" INSIDE

6'X 11" JOUR.

COAL
15 TONS

76 15/16
69 15/16

RADIAL STAYS
F. BOX 114 1/16 X 86 1/4

THROAT 13"

96" O.D.

PRESSURE
160 LBS.

82" I.D.

29 x 26

16 F.V.I.

85 O.D.

ENGS. 540-541-542

106"

86"

12'-8 3/4"

53 3/4"

48 1/4"

42 1/2"

86"

44" 44"

30"

24 1/2"

34 1/2"

10'-0"

14'-11"

155 1/2"
87 1/2"
72 1/2"
70"
6'-0"
25'-7"
38'-10 1/2"
70"
33"
72 3/4"
13'-1 1/8"
4'-6"
23 3/4"
13'-1 3/8"
9'-6"
66"
66"
66"
66"
51"
42"
18'-6"
37'-5"
76'-1 3/4"
87'-11 5/8" PULLING FACES OF COUPLERS

36"
WHEEL CTR.

R-215

C&O

318

1911

Atchison, Topeka & Santa Fe Railway NO. 3000   2-10-10-2

THE BIGGEST locomotives built up to this time were the ten Mallets of the 3000 Class which were assembled at the Santa Fe's Topeka Shops. They were designed to exert a tractive force of 111,600 pounds, an almost unbelievable power then, and were constructed from ten existing 2-10-2 engines and ten low-pressure units built by Baldwin, who also supplied the special turtle-back tenders. They were not too successful and from 1915 to 1918 were rebuilt as simple 2-10-2 types.

Builder—S.F. Topeka Shops & Baldwin Locomotive Works

Cylinders—28″ and 38″ x 32″

Weight, total—616,000 lb.

Steam Pressure—225 lb.

Dia. Drivers—57″

Tractive Effort—111,600 lb.

R.R. Class—3000

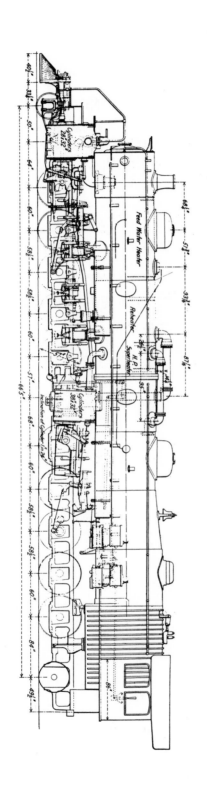

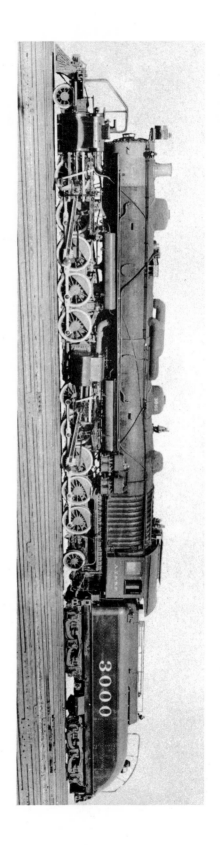

1912

New York Central Railroad NO. 3406 4-6-2

A BALDWIN engine on the New York Central is about as rare as an American Locomotive Company's machine on the Pennsylvania. This Pacific used in high-speed passenger service is one of such exceptions.

Builder—Baldwin Locomotive Works

Cylinders—23½″ x 26″

Steam Pressure—200 lb.

Fuel—16 tons

Water—10,000 gal.

Dia. Drivers—79″

Tractive Effort—30,900 lb.

R.R. Class—K3

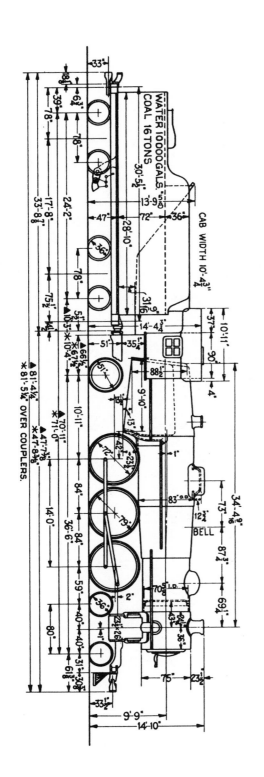

1912

Chicago, Rock Island & Pacific Railroad

NO. 2536   2-8-2

A TYPICAL FREIGHT hauler was this Mikado. It is noteworthy for its clean lines so evident in the years before various accessories contributing to efficiency were added to boilers and smokeboxes. It is probably as representative of an average 2-8-2 early in the century as might be found. The photo was taken in Philadelphia before delivery.

Builder—Baldwin Locomotive Works

Cylinders—28″ x 30″

Weight, engine—318,850

Steam Pressure—190 lb.

Fuel—16 tons or 3,200 to 4,400 gal. oil.

Water—10,000 or 11,500 gal.

Dia. Drivers—63″

Tractive Effort—60,295 lb.

R.R. Class—K60 (present)

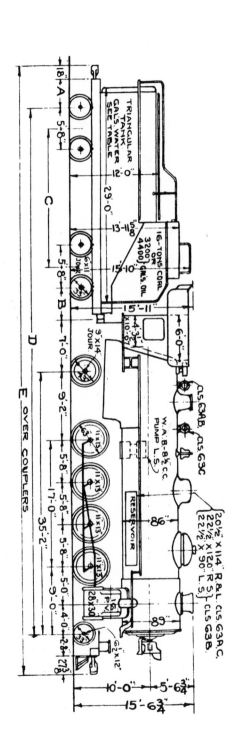

1913

Chicago, Rock Island & Pacific Railroad

NO. 961   4-6-2

TWENTY ENGINES of this type were built by the Brooks Works in 1913. As rebuilt, some were converted to oil burners and had one inch larger driving wheels. The class was also changed from P40 to P42.

Builder—American Locomotive Co.

Cylinders—25½″ x 28″

Weight, total—441,300 lb.

Steam Pressure—200 lb.

Fuel—14 tons

Water—8,500 gal.

Dia. Drivers—73″

Tractive Effort—40,250 lb.

R.R. Class (orig.)—P40 Nos. 950 to 979

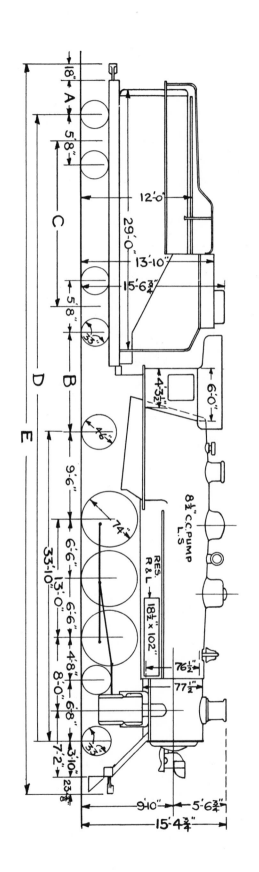

1913

Delaware, Lackawanna & Western Railroad

NO. 1156   4-6-2

THIS PACIFIC is typical of the Lackawanna's main line passenger power of the period.

Builder—American Locomotive Co.

Cylinders—25″ x 28″

Weight, total—45,600 lb.

Steam Pressure—200 lb.

Fuel—10 tons

Water—9,000 gal.

Dia. Drivers—69″

Tractive Effort—43,100 lb.

R.R. Class—N3

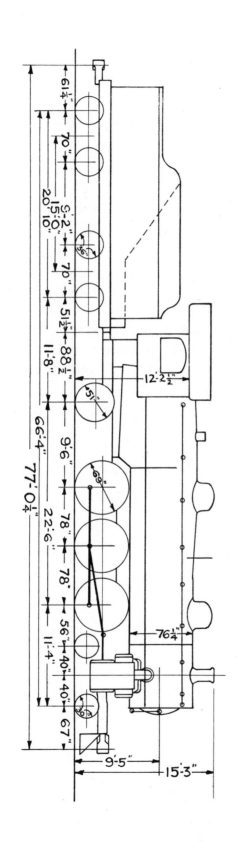

1914

Pennsylvania Railroad NO. 1737 4-6-2

THE 1737 WAS the first of one of the most famous classes of Pacifics ever operated on any railroad—the K4s. It was designed as a result of the need for greater power for passenger service, especially on the Pittsburgh Division, more than the E6s Atlantics or K2s Pacifics could produce. Essentially the engine was based on the E6s, being lengthened to take another pair of driving wheels and having larger cylinders but very similar running gear. From a rated tractive effort of 31,275 pounds for the Atlantic, an increase of about 42 per cent to 44,460 pounds was obtained in the 1737. After complete testing in service and on the Altoona test plant, the K4s was built in large numbers (at least 425) and was for many years the standard passenger locomotive on the Pennsylvania. In 1923 power-reverse gear was added and those built since had this feature; this was the only important change made, which indicates the completeness and accuracy of the original design.

Builder—Juniata Shops
Cylinders—27″ x 28″
Weight, total—468,000 lb.
Steam Pressure—205 lb.

Fuel—12½ tons
Water—7,000 gal.
Dia. Drivers—80″
Tractive Effort—44,460 lb.
R.R. Class—K4s

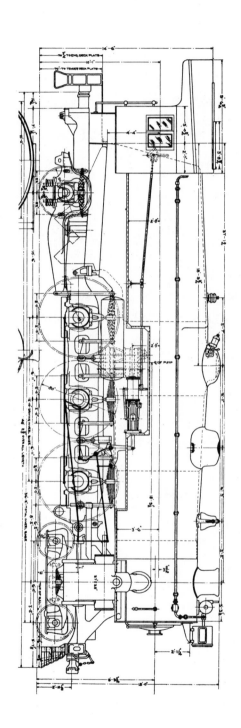

1914

Erie Railroad

NO. 5014   2-8-8-8-2

FOUR OF these giants, the only Mallets of their kind, were turned out by Baldwin's, three being for the Erie and one for the Virginian. The last had a four-wheeled truck under the tender instead of a single pair of wheels and had smaller drivers. Otherwise these "Triplexes" or "Centipedes" were similar. The 5014 was named the Matt Shay, following the Erie's custom of honoring outstanding engineers with excellent service records. After some test runs on the B. & O., she was used on the Erie's Gulf Summit grade, principally in pushing service, as were her two sister engines. None of these super engines of their day were too successful, as their poor steaming qualities were incapable of supplying enough power for their six huge cylinders. All three Erie engines were dismantled from 1929 to 1933 and the Virginian's (No. 700) was rebuilt into a 2-8-8-0 type in 1920, this reaching the end of its road in 1936.

Builder—Baldwin Locomotive Works

Cylinders—2 H.P., 2 L.P. 36" x 32"

Weight, total—864,400 lb.

Steam Pressure—210 lb.

Fuel—16 tons

Water—11,600 gal.

Dia. Drivers—63"

Tractive Effort—160,000 lb.

R.R. Class—P1

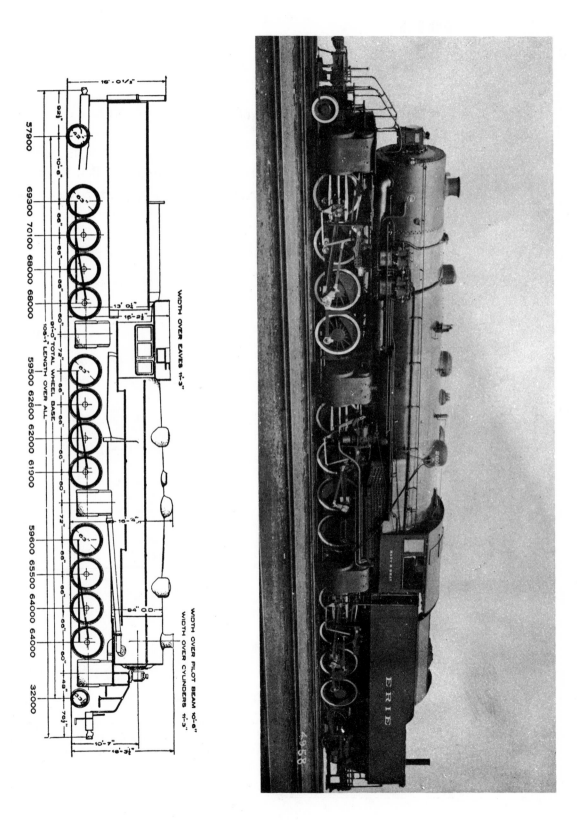

1915

St. Louis, Southwestern Railway   NO. 412   2-6-0

THIS ENGINE was formerly No. 12 on the Blytheville, Leachville and Arkansas Southern, which was acquired by the Cotton Belt Route in 1929. It represents almost the very last of the Mogul type, for records indicate that only five were built since then for use in the United States.

Builder—Baldwin Locomotive Works

Cylinders—19″ x 24″

Weight, total—169,800 lb.

Steam Pressure—170 lb.

Fuel—8 tons

Water—5,000 gal.

Dia. Drivers—54″

Tractive Effort—23,184 lb.

R.R. Class—D1-260

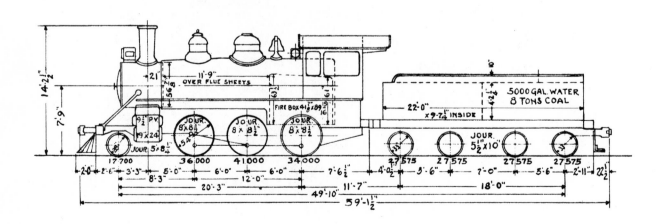

1915

Reading Company NO. 110   4-4-4

FOUR ENGINES of this type, the only ones of their kind on the Reading, were built at the company's shops. They had front and rear trucks very much alike, but being unstable were rebuilt in 1916 into Atlantics. They were renumbered 350 to 353 and reclassified as P7sa. These were particularly powerful engines for their type and were assigned to fast passenger service.

Builder—Reading Company

Cylinders—23½″ x 26″

Weight, engine—230,800 lb.

Steam Pressure—240 lb.

Dia. Drivers—80″

Tractive Effort—36,604 lb.

R.R. Class (orig.)—C1a

1916

Minneapolis & St. Louis Railway NO. 615   2-8-2

FIFTEEN ENGINES of this type were delivered in 1915 and five more, the 615 included, arrived on the M. & St. L. the following year. They were somewhat modified and partly streamlined in later years. By 1946 only six were left and diesels are replacing these.

Builder—American Locomotive Co.

Cylinders—24″ x 30″

Weight, total—448,600 lb.

Steam Pressure—200 lb.

Fuel—17½ tons (rebuilt tender)

Water—10,200 gal.

Dia. Drivers—59″

Tractive Effort—49,800 lb.

R.R. Class—MAC1

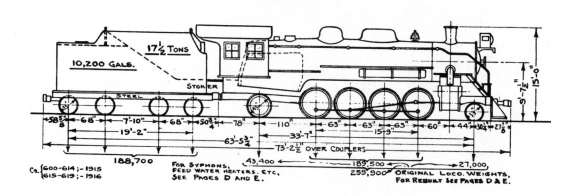

1917

Reading Company

THIRTY-ONE Mallets of this type were built for the Reading from 1917 to 1919. All were compounds, but for increased starting tractive power they could use steam at reduced pressure as single-expansion engines. The first eleven locomotives of this class were rebuilt at the company's shops as 2-10-2 types (K1sa and K1sc) from 1927 to 1930. By 1936 the 1811, 1816, 1818, and 1821 were rebuilt with single-expansion cylinders and by 1945 the remaining Mallets had been similarly rebuilt, making these articulateds the most powerful locomotives in service on the Reading.

Builder—Baldwin Locomotive Works

Cylinders—26″ and 40″ x 32″

Weight, total—478,500 lb.

Steam Pressure—210 lb.

Dia. Drivers—55½″

Tractive Effort—
  (orig.)—98,480 lb.
  (rebuilt)—111,400 lb.

R.R. Class—(orig.)—N1sa
  (rebuilt)—N1sd

1918

Chesapeake & Ohio Railway

NO. 137   4-8-2

EIGHT MONTHS after the United States entered World War I the government took over control of all trunk-line railroads, and their operation was put under the United States Railroad Administration. The Administration created a committee to standardize locomotive specifications, with the result that twelve freight and passenger designs divided among eight types were prepared. The Baldwin, American, and Lima Companies shared in building these standard engines, one of which is represented by this Chesapeake & Ohio Mountain type.

Builder—Baldwin Locomotive Works

Cylinders—28" x 30"

Weight, total—546,000 lb.

Steam Pressure—200 lb.

Fuel—16 tons

Water—10,000 gal.

Dia. Drivers—69"

Tractive Effort—58,000 lb.

1918

Chicago & Eastern Illinois Railroad   NO. 1925   2-8-2

AMONG THE United States Railroad Administration standard designs were light and heavy Mikados. This C. & E.I. locomotive was one of the former.

Builder—American Locomotive Co.

Cylinders—26″ x 30″

Weight, total—477,400 lb.

Steam Pressure—200 lb.

Fuel—16 tons

Water—10,000 gal.

Dia. Drivers—63″

Tractive Effort—54,700 lb.

R.R. Class—N2

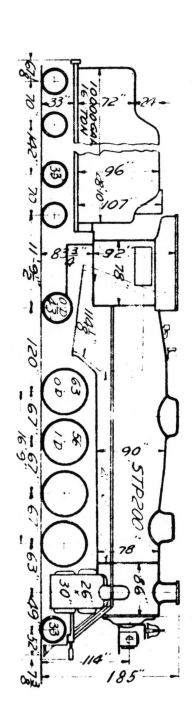

1918

Pennsylvania Railroad

NO. 7246   2-10-2

THIS Santa Fe type was designed to handle heavy ore and coal trains on lines west of Pittsburgh, its class being N1s. The N2s were U.S.R.A. designs of which thirty were acquired and also assigned to the same division. The N1s locomotives were among the most powerful 2-10-2 types ever built.

Builder—American Locomotive Co. (35)
Baldwin Locomotive Works (25)

Cylinders—30″ x 32″

Weight, total—642,000 lb.

Steam Pressure—215 lb.

Fuel—20 tons

Water—10,000 gal.

Dia. Drivers—62″

Tractive Effort—84,890 lb.

R.R. Class—N1s

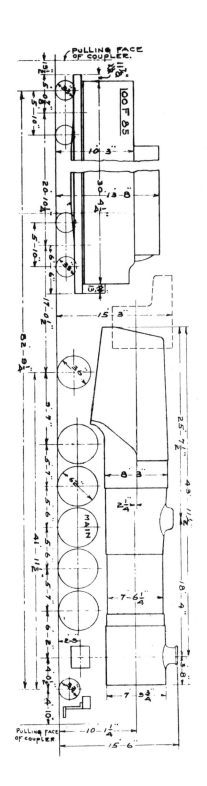

Louisville & Nashville Railroad   NO. 1462   2-8-2

THIS MIKADO was one of eighteen locomotives built by the road's South Louisville Shops in 1918 and 1919. They were somewhat larger than the preceding J1 type and were stoker fired. Another sixteen (J2A) 2-8-2's, also company-built, followed in 1921, and the last order for this type was for twenty-four J4A engines delivered by Baldwin's in 1929.

Builder—Louisville & Nashville   *Fuel*—16 tons

Cylinders—28″ x 30″   *Water*—9,000 gal.

Weight, total—501,000 lb.   *Dia. Drivers*—60″

Steam Pressure—195 lb.   *Tractive Effort*—65,000 lb.

R.R. Class—J2

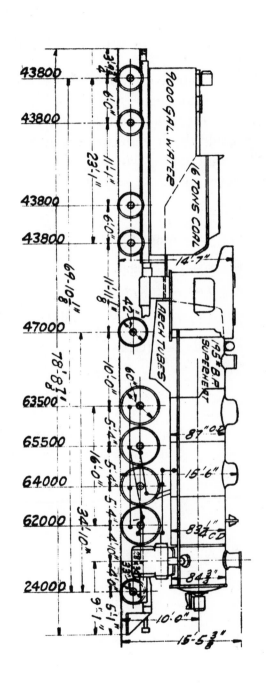

1919

Pennsylvania Railroad NO. 3700 2-8-8-0

ONE OF the most interesting articulated locomotives ever built was this single-expansion type, the most powerful steam engine the Pennsylvania has ever had. The drawbar pull was too great to handle trains not fully equipped with the latest MCB couplers, and this locomotive was used in pushing service on the Allegheny Mountain grades, where it performed very well. No others of its type were ever built, but valuable data was obtained during its ten years of service.

Builder—Juniata Shops

Cylinders—30½" x 32"

Weight, total—814,000 lb.

Steam Pressure—205 lb.

Fuel—14 tons

Water—13,000 gal.

Dia. Drivers—62"

Tractive Effort—135,000 lb.

R.R. Class—HC1s

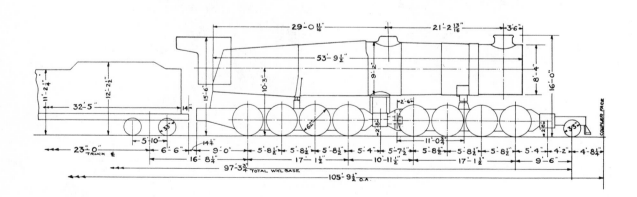

1920

Illinois Central Railroad

NO. 2814   2-10-2

HERE IS a locomotive used in fast freight service on the Iowa Division of the Illinois Central. Two different domes, a front end throttle, and mechanical lubricator appear to be the only visible external changes made on this engine since it was first put into service. Originally in the 2901 to 3025 series, it was renumbered as shown when rebuilt.

Builder—Lima Locomotive Works

Cylinders—30" x 32"

Weight, total—631,500 lb.

Steam Pressure—275 lb.

Fuel—19 tons

Water—12,000 gal.

Dia. Drivers—64½"

Tractive Effort—110,512 lb.

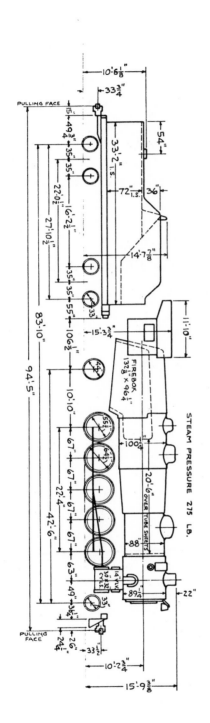

1921

Atchison, Topeka & Santa Fe Railway   NO. 4000   2-8-2

THERE WERE one hundred and one locomotives of this class built from 1921 to 1926, the first of the series and No. 4015 of 1923 being illustrated. More Mikados are represented in the company's roster among twentieth-century freight power than any other type.

Builder—Baldwin Locomotive Works

Cylinders—27″ x 32″

Weight, Engine—330,500 lb.

Steam Pressure—200 lb.

Dia. Drivers—63″

Tractive Effort—63,000 lb.

R.R. Class—4000

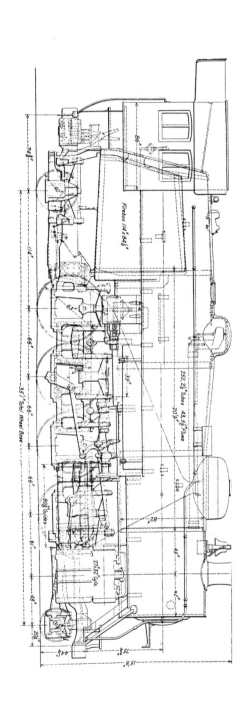

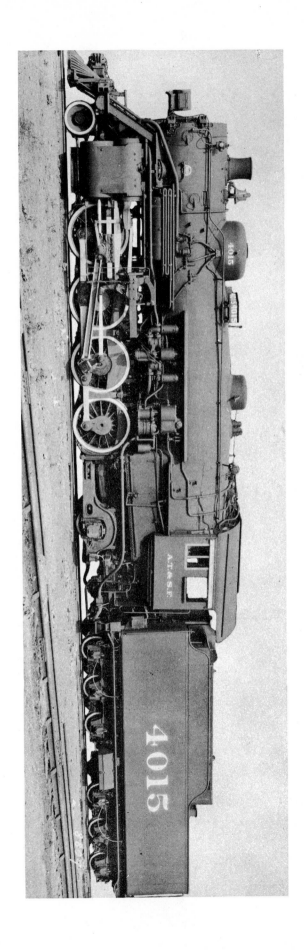

Louisville & Nashville Railroad   NO. 255   4-6-2

THE FIRST five Pacifics were used on the L. & N. in 1907. They were Alco engines and classed as K1. Forty-five more were built by the company shops up to 1910 (K2A). Following these came the seventeen K3 Class in 1912 and 1913, and forty-six of the K4 Class from 1914 to 1922, all company-built. Other classifications including U.S.R.A. engines (K5) following up to 1925 were eight Baldwin-built K5's, an Alco K4, and four K6 engines.

Builder—Louisville & Nashville   *Fuel*—16 tons

Cylinders—22″ x 28″   *Water*—9,000 gal.

Weight, total—412,000 lb.   *Dia. Drivers*—69″

Steam Pressure—200 lb.   *Tractive Effort*—33,400 lb.

                                      R.R. Class—K4B

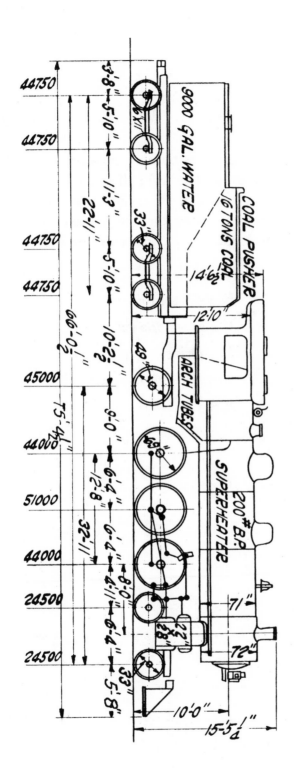

9000 GAL. WATER

COAL PUSHER

16 TONS COAL

ARCH TUBES

200# B.P. SUPERHEATER

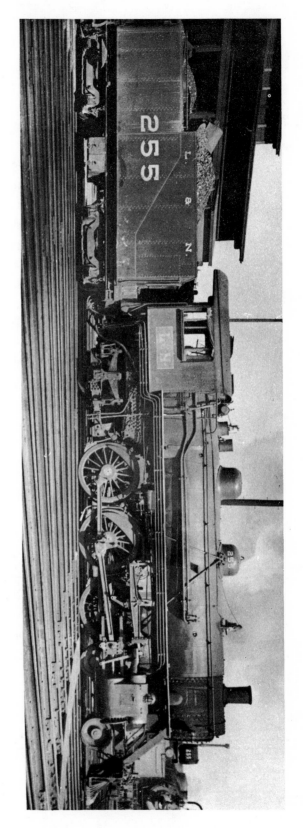

1923

Pennsylvania Railroad

NO. 6813   4-8-2

THE FIRST Mountain type on the P.R.R. was built experimentally at Altoona in 1923 and was numbered 4700. The 6813 illustrates this class, although it was built somewhat later. In 1930 the latest development of the 4-8-2 on the P.R.R., the M1a, was built. Its appearance is generally similar to the M1 but it has larger tenders. All these locomotives have been used in both passenger and fast freight service.

Builder—Juniata Shops

Cylinders—27″ x 30″

Weight, total—560,000 lb.

Steam Pressure—250 lb.

Fuel—15¾ tons

Water—7,700 gal.

Dia. Drivers—72″

Tractive Effort—64,550 lb.

R.R. Class—M1

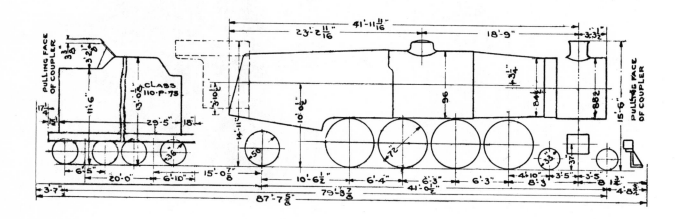

1923

Missouri Pacific Railroad

NO. 1430   2-8-2

ONCE POPULAR in freight service on the Mo.Pac. (one hundred and seventy-one were used until recently), this type of locomotive has performed economically over years of operation. They are still used for every kind of freight handling although, as with most other roads, diesels are replacing them. Some of this class were oil burners and about half were booster-equipped.

Builder—American Locomotive Co.

Cylinders—27" x 32"

Weight, engine—305,115 lb.

Steam Pressure—200 lb.

Dia. Drivers—63"

Tractive Effort—
engine—62,950 lb.
booster—4,475 lb.

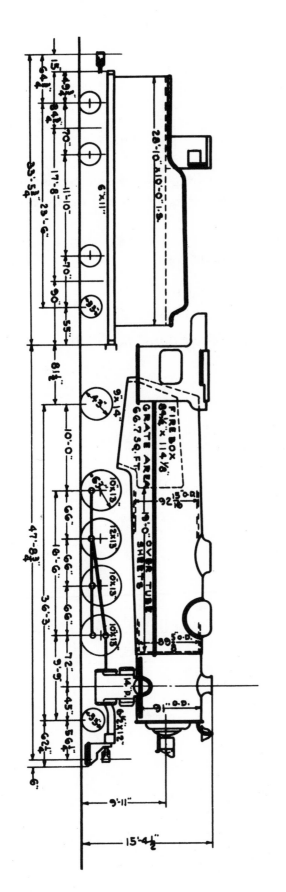

1923

Illinois Central Railroad   NO. 1986   2-8-2

THIS IS A heavy Mikado which was used in freight service on the Kentucky Division. It has been rebuilt with larger cylinders and its present number is 1474.

Builder—Baldwin Locomotive Works

Cylinders—27″ x 30″

Weight, total—525,000 lb.

Steam Pressure—225 lb.

Fuel—16 tons

Water—13,000 gal.

Dia. Drivers—63½″

Tractive Effort—69,743 lb.

1923

Northern Pacific Railway

NO. 1844   2-8-2

THE 1844 WAS the Mikado which in 1925 set a world record for long-distance freight runs by hauling a full tonnage freight from the Pacific Coast to the Twin Cities without uncoupling from its train. Locomotives of this class—the W5—were the Northern Pacific's heaviest 2-8-2's and were originally assigned to the Yellowstone Division, where the ruling grade is about 1 per cent in both directions, until the big Z5 articulateds replaced them. The 1844 was photographed at Muir, Montana, in November, 1940, just after it had helped a time freight to the top of Bozeman Pass. It is presently assigned to the Lake Superior Division and is one of twenty-five such engines originally ordered.

Builder—American Locomotive Co.

Cylinders—28″ x 30″

Weight, total—545,100 lb.

Steam Pressure—200 lb.

Fuel—16 tons

Water—10,000 gal.

Dia. Drivers—63″

Tractive Effort—63,460 lb.

R.R. Class—W5 Nos. 1835 to 1859

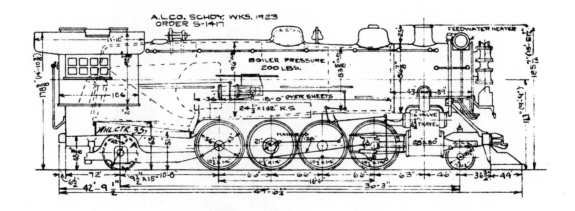

1924

Lehigh Valley Railroad

NO. 2092   4-6-2

TEN OF these locomotives replacing lighter Pacifics were delivered in 1924 and two more built in the company's shops were put in service the following year. They were used for heavy passenger traffic between Newark and Buffalo, handling without assistance trains of nine cars between Mauch Chunk and Glen Summit Springs, where the grades are 69 feet to the mile. They are fully modern 4-6-2's in that they are equipped with boosters, stokers, and superheaters.

Builder—American Locomotive Co.

Cylinders—25″ x 28″

Weight, total—533,900 lb.

Fuel—22 tons

Water—12,000 gal.

Dia. Drivers—77″

Tractive Effort—
engine—41,534 lb.
booster—10,400 lb.

R.R. Class—K6B

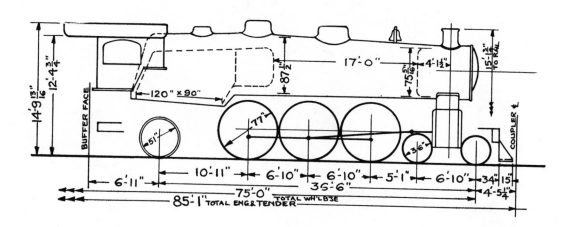

1924

Maine Central Railroad

NO. 469   4-6-2

MOST MAIN-LINE passenger service on the Maine Central was handled by these Pacifics until the Class D Hudsons were delivered in 1930, and even the latter in turn are being replaced by diesels for this traffic.

Builder—American Locomotive Co.

Cylinders—24″ x 28″

Weight, total—470,900 lb.

Steam Pressure—195 lb.

Fuel—13¼ tons

Water—9,100 gal.

Dia. Drivers—73″

Tractive Effort—
engine—36,500 lb.
booster—10,300 lb.

R.R. Class—C₃b

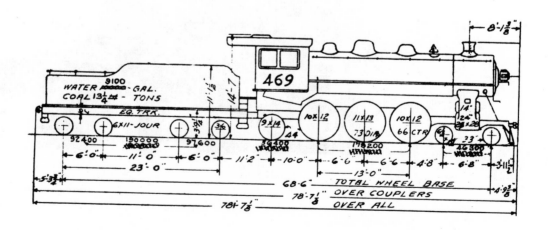

1925

Lima Locomotive Works NO. 1 2-8-4

THIS WAS ONE of another new wheel arrangement locomotives which was given the name Berkshire. The first was originally No. 1 when built by the Lima Locomotive Works for experimental use and was owned by them until purchased by the Illinois Central. It has been called the forerunner of all super-power locomotives and the basis in fundamental design of most steam main-line engines built since. The principal objectives were to obtain high horsepower capacity and improved economy of fuel, which aims were fully attained. Its design was based largely on the experimental Mikado No. 8000 of 1922, built for the New York Central.

Builder—Lima Locomotive Works

Cylinders—28″ x 30″

Weight, engine—385,000 lb.

Steam Pressure—240 lb.

Fuel—21 tons

Water—15,500 gal.

Dia. Drivers—63″

Tractive Effort—
engine—69,400 lb.
booster—13,200 lb.

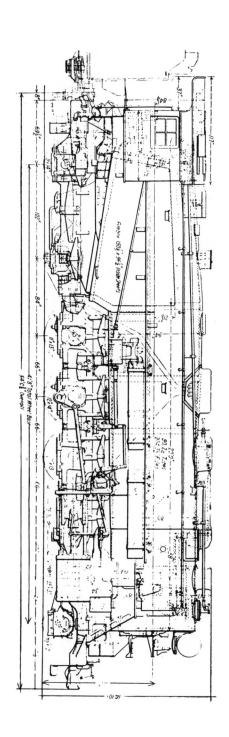

1925

Texas & Pacific Railway

NO. 600   2-10-4

THE 600 WAS one of the first ten locomotives of their wheel arrangement. The type taking the name Texas for the T. & P. In heavy freight service they proved so satisfactory that fifteen more were ordered in 1927, thirty in 1928, and another fifteen in 1929.

Builder—Lima Locomotive Works

Cylinders—29″ x 32″

Weight, total—723,200 lb.

Steam Pressure—250 lb.

Fuel—5,000 gal. oil

Water—14,000 gal.

Dia. Drivers—63″

Tractive Effort—
engine—83,000 lb.
booster—13,000 lb.

R.R. Class—I1

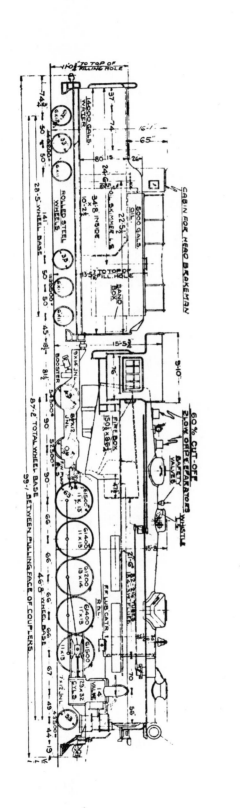

1925

Canadian National Railways   NO. 6038   4-8-2

THE 6038 WAS one of five Mountain types delivered to the Canadian National, then called the Grand Trunk Western. The photo shows the locomotive's original appearance; in the course of rebuildings since then, smoke deflectors, Boxpok driving wheels, stokers, mechanical lubricators, and other equipment have been applied.

Builder—Baldwin Locomotive Works

Cylinders—26" x 30"

Weight, total—604,110 lb.

Steam Pressure—210 lb.

Fuel—18 tons

Water—13,500 gal.

Dia. Drivers—73"

Tractive Effort—49,600 lb.

R.R. Class—U1c

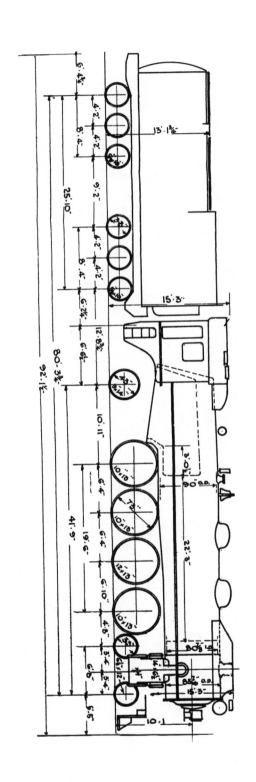

1926

Chesapeake & Ohio Railway

NO. 1572   2-8-8-2

By about the early twenties the trend from true Mallets to high-pressure or single-expansion articulateds was well established. The 1572 was one of a second group of twenty such locomotives built by Baldwin's for the C. & O., the first twenty-five having been built in 1924 by Alco. Tunnel clearances had prevented the use of larger compounds with their huge low-pressure cylinders, so this type of single-expansion engine was developed to meet the need for motive power with greater capacity. The Baldwin locomotives were essentially the same as the first series (H7), except that they had larger tenders. Upon delivery they went first into service between Russell, Kentucky, and Columbus, Ohio, where they made the 113 miles in five hours actual running time with trains of 9,500 tons. They averaged about 4,400 miles a month and their coal consumption averaged only 39 pounds per 1,000 gross ton miles.

Builder—Baldwin Locomotive Works

Cylinders (4)—23″ x 32″

Weight, total—868,900 lb.

Steam Pressure—205 lb.

Fuel—20 tons

Water—16,000 gal.

Dia. Drivers—57″

Tractive Effort—103,500 lb.

R.R. Class—H7A

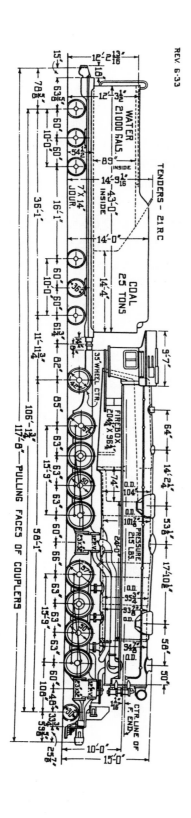

1926

Union Pacific Railroad

NO. 9085   4-12-2

CALLED THE Union Pacific type, these were the first of their kind and the largest non-articulated locomotives ever built, having the longest driving wheel base—30 feet 8 inches—ever designed. They were developed "to haul mile-long freights at passenger-train speed." There were eighty-eight of these three-cylinder engines of 4,330 horsepower, and when they were first placed in service they were said to deliver more ton miles at less expense than any other prevailing type of steam locomotive.

Builder—American Locomotive Co.

Cylinders—27" x 32", (1) 27" x 31"

Weight, total—782,000 lb.

Steam Pressure—220 lb.

Fuel—21 tons

Water—15,000 gal.

Dia. Drivers—67"

Tractive Effort—96,650 lb.

1926

Baldwin Locomotive Works   NO. 60,000   4-10-2

THE 60,000 WAS an experimental high-pressure three-cylinder compound locomotive with a water tube firebox. Incorporating the latest in modern design, this engine was loaned to a number of roads for tests. Among these were the Pennsylvania, Baltimore & Ohio, Chicago, Burlington & Quincy, Atchison, Topeka & Santa Fe, Southern Pacific, and Great Northern.

In 1933 after these trials, it was sent to the Franklin Institute in Philadelphia where it has been permanently set up for exhibition on a special flooring demonstrating six types of bridge construction. As its number indicates, it was the 60,000th locomotive turned out by the Baldwin Works.

Builder—Baldwin Locomotive
   Works
Cylinders (2)—27″ x 32″,
   (1) 27″ x 32″
Weight, total—700,900 lb.
Steam Pressure—350 lb.

Fuel—16 tons
Water—12,000 gal.
Dia. Drivers—63½″
Tractive Effort—82,500 lb.

New York Central Railroad NO. 5297 4-6-4

THROUGH THE late twenties and early thirties, the Hudsons, first passenger engines of their wheel arrangement, were the pride of the New York Central. They were markedly superior to the Pacifics previously used in this service in both capacity and efficiency and were assigned to hauling the Central's famous "steel fleet," including the Twentieth Century Limited, the Empire State, the Wolverine, and similar well-known trains. Nearly two hundred were built, some of the later designs having several types of streamlining. No. 5200 was the first of the series built in 1927, and the photo is of a 1930 engine.

5200

Builder—American Locomotive Co.

Cylinders—25″ x 28″

Weight, total—565,200 lb.

Steam Pressure—225 lb.

Fuel—17 tons

Water—10,000 gal.

Dia. Drivers—79″

Tractive Effort—
engine—42,300 lb.
booster—10,900 lb.

R.R. Class—J1

5297

Builder—American Locomotive Co.

Cylinders—22½″ x 29″

Weight, total—671,800 lb.

Steam Pressure—275 lb.

Fuel—28 tons

Water—13,600 gal.

Dia. Drivers—79″

Tractive Effort—
engine—43,440 lb.
booster—12,100 lb.

R.R. Class—J1c

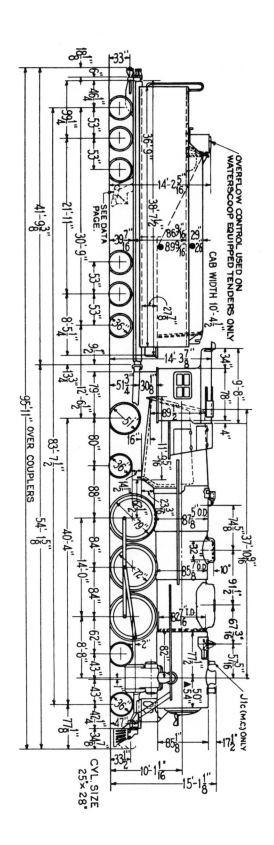

1927

Richmond, Fredericksburg &
Potomac Railroad

NO. 325   4-6-2

THESE LOCOMOTIVES were particularly handsome examples of the Pacific type and when built were among the most powerful of their wheel arrangement in service. They were stoker-fired and although they originally had 210-pound steam pressure with a tractive power of 48,580 pounds, this has been increased with resulting improved traction. They were used for the heaviest passenger service.

Builder—Baldwin Locomotive
    Works
Cylinders—27″ x 28″
Weight, total—532,000 lb.
Steam Pressure—225 lb.

Fuel—16 tons
Water—10,000 gal.
Dia. Drivers—75″
Tractive Effort—52,050 lb.

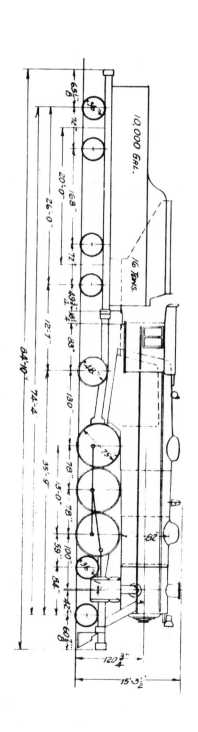

1927

Illinois Central Railroad   NO. 3540   0-8-0

HERE IS A typical eight-wheeled switcher of the late twenties. It was one of an order for fifteen (Nos. 3540 to 3554) and is still in service at the East St. Louis Terminal.

Builder—Baldwin Locomotive
    Works

Cylinders—25″ x 28″

Weight, total—380,200 lb.

Steam Pressure—190 lb.

Fuel—9 tons

Water—9,000 gal.

Dia. Drivers—53″

Tractive Effort—56,462 lb.

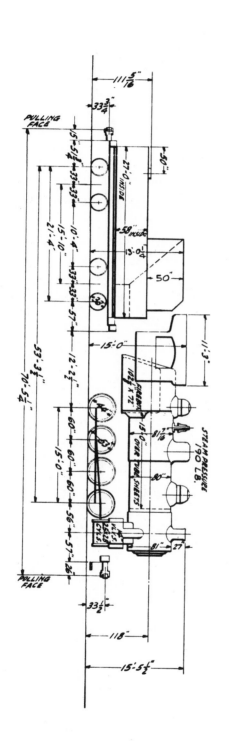

1927

Denver & Rio Grande Western Railroad

NO. 3603   2-8-8-2

TEN OF THESE articulateds went into freight service in August and September of 1927. They were especially designed for road and pushing service on the Salida Division, which crosses the Continental Divide at an elevation of 10,240 feet and includes the most difficult operating section of the main line. The maximum grade on the east slope of the Rockies is 1.42 per cent and that on the west is 3 per cent. On these grades one of these locomotives is rated at 3,300 tons on the east slope and 1,400 tons on the west.

Builder—American Locomotive Co.

Cylinders—26" x 32"

Weight, total—992,500 lb.

Steam Pressure—240 lb.

Fuel—30 tons

Water—18,000 gal.

Dia. Drivers—63"

Tractive Effort—131,800 lb.

R.R. Class—1–131
Nos. 3600 to 3609

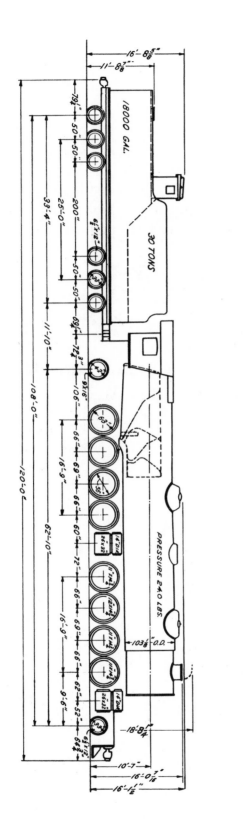

1927

Chicago, Burlington &
Quincy Railroad

NO. 6318   2-10-4

TEN LOCOMOTIVES of this type were placed in service in 1927 and two more by 1929. They are excellent examples of the Texas type, which the Burlington has used for heavy freight traffic. Their performance has been very satisfactory.

Builder—Baldwin Locomotive Works

Cylinders—28″ x 32″

Weight, total—890,370 lb.

Steam Pressure—250 lb.

Fuel—24 tons

Water—21,500 gal.

Dia. Drivers—64″

Tractive Effort—83,300 lb.

R.R. Class—M4a

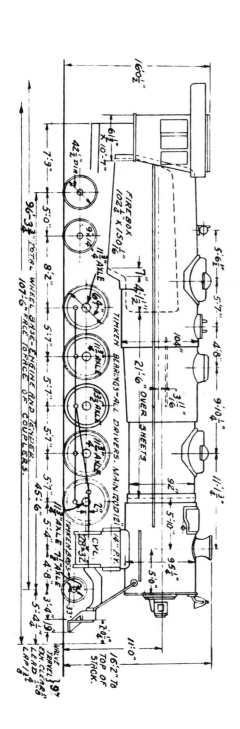

1928

Boston & Albany Railroad   NO. 400   4-6-6 T

THESE DOUBLE-ENDERS were designed for suburban service out of Boston to Brookline Junction where no turntable was available. Five engines of this type were built and they were capable of handling ten steel cars. They were the last tank engines built for this type of traffic.

Builder—American Locomotive Co.

Cylinders—23½″ x 26″

Weight, total—352,000 lb.

Steam Pressure—215 lb.

Fuel—6 tons

Water—5,000 gal.

Dia. Drivers—63″

Tractive Effort—41,600 lb.

R.R. Class—D1a

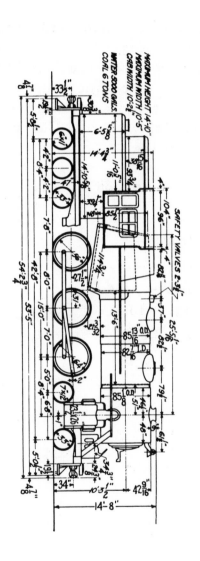

1928

Texas & Pacific Railway   NO. 909   4-8-2

THERE WERE five of these Mountain-type locomotives in this order, successors to an earlier five (M1) built by Alco in 1925. The first five had been so successful in handling the heaviest passenger traffic that these Baldwin machines were added to the roster. They were particularly good-looking engines having polished rods and valve gear, nickel-plated cylinder, and steam chest covers, and they were highly finished. Their performance was fully as good as their fine appearance.

Builder—Baldwin Locomotive Works

Cylinders—27" x 30"

Weight, total—654,300 lb.

Steam Pressure—225 lb.

Fuel—6,000 gal. oil

Water—14,000 gal.

Dia. Drivers—73"

Tractive effort—
    engine—57,300 lb.
    booster—10,450

R.R. Class—M2

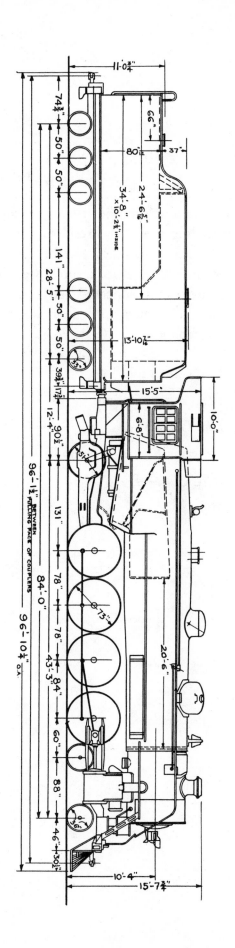

1928

Baltimore & Ohio Railroad   NO. 5320   4-6-2

ALTHOUGH SIMILAR in general specifications to the twenty other President-class (P7) Pacifics of the preceding year, the President Cleveland had Caprotti valve gear and varied in some details, noticeably in external features. Its lines and finish were markedly British, and to attain this simplicity in appearance the air compressor was located between the frames and the piping was generally hung from the runboards. It was the only locomotive of this type and was later converted to Class P9A.

Builder—Baltimore & Ohio

Cylinders—27″ x 28″

Weight, total—569,500 lb.

Steam Pressure—230 lb.

Fuel—17½ tons

Water—12,000 gal.

Dia. Drivers—80″

Tractive Effort—50,000 lb.

R.R. Class—P9

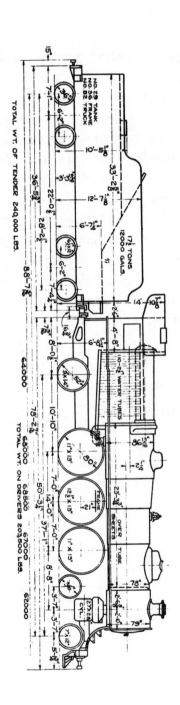

1929

Minneapolis, St. Paul &
Saulte Ste. Marie Railroad   NO. 4018   4-8-2

BUILT AT THE road's Shoreham Shops in 1929 and 1930, the three locomotives of this type cost $85,000 each to construct. According to the *Minneapolis Journal* (Dec. 29, 1929): "Proud in a new coat of shiny black and looking as neat and trim and fast as a thoroughbred, No. 4018 was rolled out of the shops at the Soo Line yards Saturday before an admiring throng. . . . This new locomotive, this No. 4018, is the first railway engine ever built in Minneapolis. It will be followed by others, one of which is nearly done and another of which is just started. While the Soo Line officials take great pride in having constructed such a machine here, they find greater satisfaction in the knowledge such construction has served to prevent the seasonal layoff of mechanics. It has meant a continuance of payrolls, with resulting better conditions in homes."

Builder—Soo Line

Cylinders—27" x 30"

Weight, total—549,100 lb.

Steam Pressure—200 lb.

Fuel—17½ tons

Water—12,000 gal.

Dia. Drivers—69"

Tractive Effort—
engine—53,900 lb.
booster—10,000 lb.

R.R. Class—N20

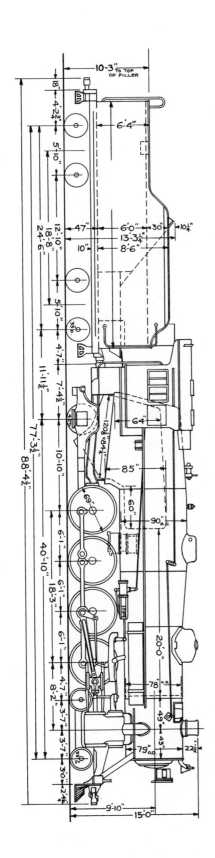

1929

Great Northern Railway

NO. 2552   4-8-4

No. 2552 WAS one of the first six Northern-type locomotives to be purchased by the Great Northern. They replaced Mountain-type (P2) power and were used to haul the Empire Builder, new this year on a schedule more than five hours faster than the existing timetable called for. They could handle fourteen passenger cars up the 1.8 per cent grades in the Rockies without helpers both eastbound and westbound and had more tractive power than the S2 engines which followed. The latter had then the largest driving wheels—80 inches—of any Northern type and were used for fast running on the more level stretches.

Builder—Baldwin Locomotive Works

Cylinders—28″ x 30″

Weight, total—847,900 lb.

Steam Pressure—250 lb.

Fuel—5,800 gal. oil (except 2552-coal burner)

Water—22,000 gal.

Dia. Drivers—73″

Tractive Effort—67,000 lb.

R.R. Class—S1

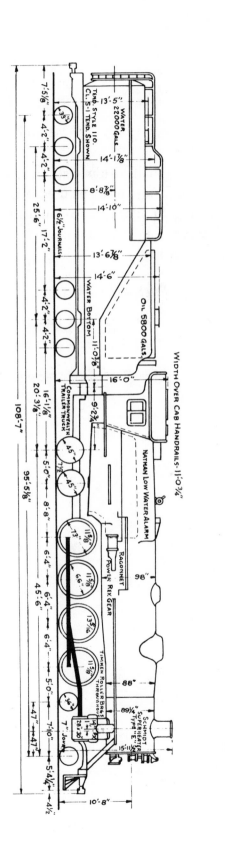

1929

Southern Railway

NO. 1407   4-6-2

THERE WERE five of these Pacifics originally—especially noteworthy for their trim lines and beautiful finish. They were painted a bright apple green with gold lettering and striping. Similar engines, built by Alco, followed, those assigned to the Crescent Limited having a crescent on the cylinders and the train's name on the tender.

Builder—Baldwin Locomotive Works

Cylinders—27″ x 28″

Weight, total—526,600 lb.

Steam Pressure—210 lb.

Fuel—16 tons

Water—12,000 gal.

Dia. Drivers—73″

Tractive Effort—45,000 lb.

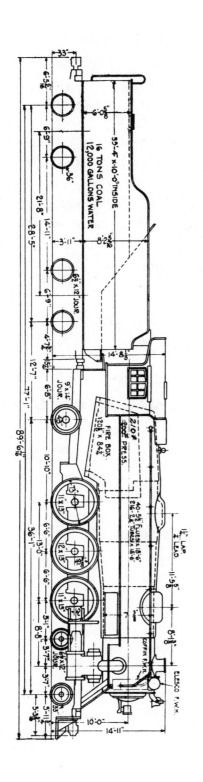

1929

Delaware & Hudson Railroad   NO. 652   4-6-2

IN APPEARANCE this Pacific is even more "Anglicized" than the B. & O.'s President Cleveland (page 165). Built at the D. & H. Shops at Colonie, New York, it followed British practice in design in that all pipes and fittings were covered by the boiler jacket. The headlight generator, air compressors, and power reverse gear were located under the boiler and between the frames. The headlight was recessed into the center of the smokebox door. The 652 was used in passenger service between Troy, New York, and Montreal, Quebec.

Builder—Delaware & Hudson

Cylinders—20″ x 28″

Weight, total—443,800 lb.

Steam Pressure—260 lb.

Fuel—14 tons

Water—11,000 gal.

Dia. Drivers—73″

Tractive Effort—41,600 lb.

R.R. Class—P1

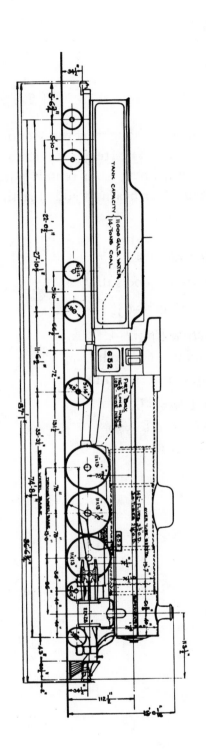

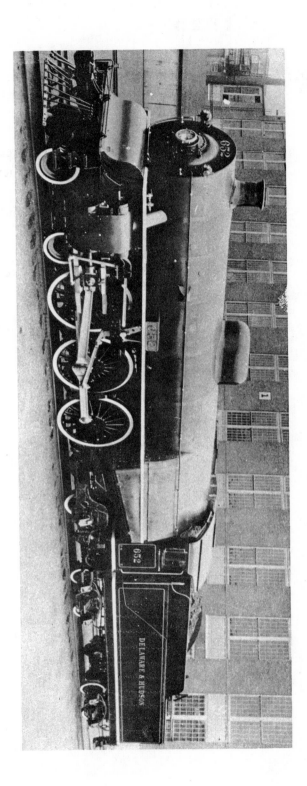

1929

Chicago, Indianapolis & Louisville Railway

NO. 573   2-8-2

THE 573 WAS one of the last new steam locomotives bought by the Monon. There were ten in this class and they were used in fast freight service between Lafayette and Youngtown, Kentucky. They were rebuilt with boosters and feedwater heaters, and five had roller bearings added at the Lafayette Shops.

Builder—American Locomotive Co.

Cylinders—27″ x 32″

Weight, total—565,500 lb.

Steam Pressure—220 lb.

Fuel—20 tons

Water—12,000 gal.

Dia. Drivers—63″

Tractive Effort—
engine—69,240 lb.
booster—11,500 lb.

R.R. Class—J4
Nos. 570 to 579

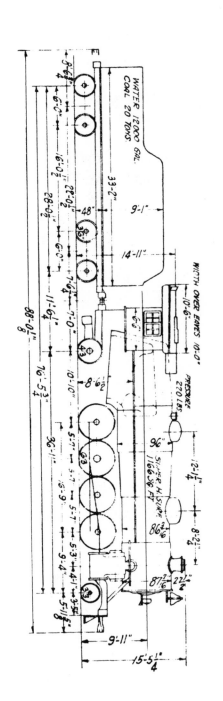

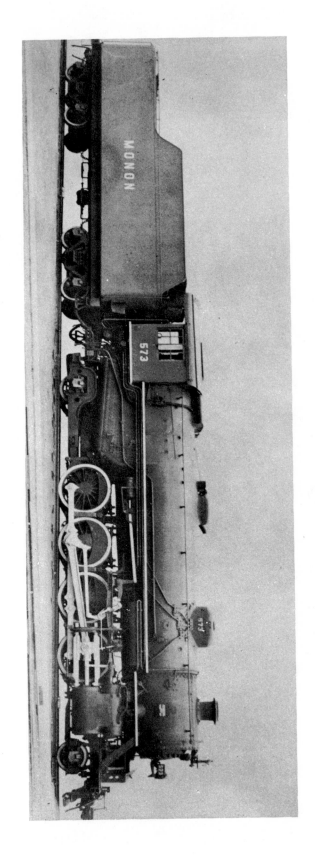

1929

Southern Railway

NO. 4052   2-8-8-2

THE 4052 WAS one of eight articulateds ordered as the result of the satisfactory performance of a similar engine built experimentally in 1926. These locomotives have been used in the heaviest freight service such as on the 4.5 per cent Saluda grade in western North Carolina, the Southern operating until recent years a sizable fleet of articulated power.

Builder—Baldwin Locomotive
　Works
Cylinders—23″ x 30″
Weight, total—660,400 lb.
Steam Pressure—210 lb.

Fuel—16 tons
Water—10,000 gal.
Dia. Drivers—57″
Tractive Effort—96,000 lb.

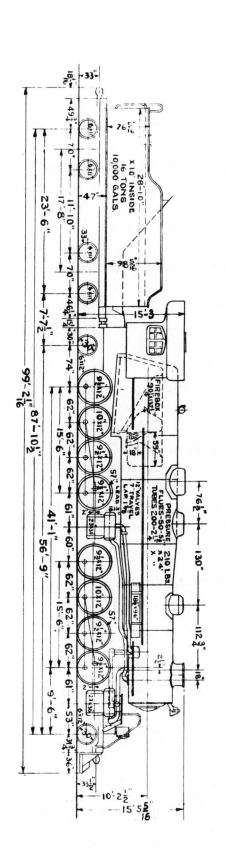

1930

Timken Roller Bearing Company NO. 1111 4-8-4

THE TIMKEN "Four Aces" was built for the purpose of demonstrating the importance and use of roller bearings on all axle journals of steam locomotives. Rather than rebuild an existing engine, a new one was built so that it could be impartially tested by any interested railroads. Fifty manufacturers of locomotive appliances co-operated with Timken in the project, with a 4-8-4 type being chosen, this to have a top speed of 85 miles an hour.

Upon completion the 1111 was first operated in freight service on the New York Central. From there it was tried in both passenger and freight service on thirteen other roads. In these trials some well-known trains such as the C. & O.'s Sportsman and the New Haven's Merchants Limited were hauled by the 1111. On the Pennsylvania it handled twelve passenger cars up the Allegheny mountain grade without a helper and even saved three minutes on the standard schedule. It fully justified the claims for roller bearings and after these service tests totaling 88,992 miles were completed by August, 1931, it was delivered to the Northern Pacific. After this road had tried it, the Four Aces was purchased by them in February, 1933. Renumbered the 2626, it was used for passenger traffic on Trains 1 and 2 between Seattle and Yakima and later between Seattle and Missoula, Montana.

Builder—American Locomotive Co.

Cylinders—27″ x 30″

Weight, total—711,500 lb.

Steam Pressure—250 lb.

Fuel—21 tons

Water—14,550 gal.

Dia. Drivers—73″

Tractive Effort—63,700 lb.

N.P. R.R. Class—A1

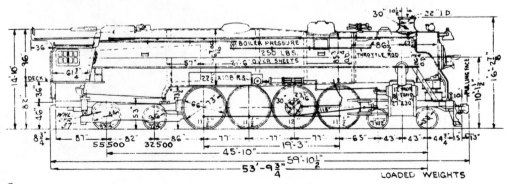

LOADED WEIGHTS

1930

Chicago, Milwaukee, St. Paul & Pacific Railroad

NO. 6402   4-6-4

IN APRIL of this year, fourteen of these Hudsons were received and placed in service on the most important trains between Chicago and the Twin Cities, replacing lighter Pacifics. They had modern appliances such as stokers and mechanical and pressure lubrication which, with large capacity tenders, allowed the 420-mile run to be made without terminal attention en route.

On Friday July 20, 1934, the 6402 with a five-car train smashed the world's record for sustained steam train speed. The train was the regularly scheduled 9 A.M. Milwaukee Express for which the running time had been reduced on July 15 to 90 minutes for the Chicago–Milwaukee trip. Most of the passengers were unaware that a record run was to be attempted until about five miles out of Chicago when the engineer opened the throttle and the high speed became evident. The entire run of 85.7 miles was made in 67 minutes, 35 seconds, or at 76.07 miles an hour. Between Mayfair and Lake—68.9 miles—the train broke all existing records for the distance with an average speed of 89.92 miles an hour. The highest speed recorded by the speedometer was 103.5 miles an hour at Oakwood.

Builder—Baldwin Locomotive Works
Cylinders—26" x 28"
Weight, total—653,650 lb.
Steam Pressure—225 lb.

Fuel—20 tons
Water—15,000 gal.
Dia. Drivers—80"
Tractive Effort—45,250 lb.
R.R. Class—F6

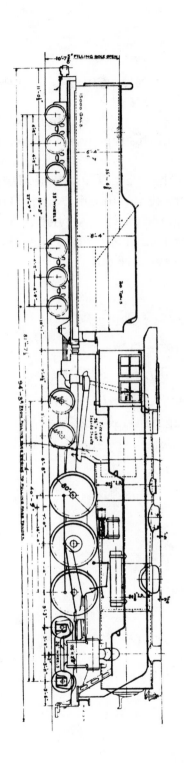

Northern Pacific Railway   NO. 5002   2-8-8-4

IN 1928 THE Northern Pacific's first 2-8-8-4, the 5000, was built by Alco, and after very successful trials eleven more of this type were ordered from Baldwin's. For years these Yellowstones were the world's largest locomotives and they still remain near the top in this class. They were designed to haul 4,000-ton trains the 216 miles between Mandan, North Dakota, and Glendive, Montana, up 1.1 per cent grades, which service they have performed most satisfactorily. Some improvements such as the addition of roller bearings have been made and their tractive power as last reported was 145,930 pounds.

Builder—Baldwin Locomotive Works

Cylinders (4)—26″ x 32″

Weight, total—1,125,400 lb.

Steam Pressure—250 lb.

Fuel—27 tons

Water—21,200 gal.

Dia. Drivers—63″

Tractive Effort (orig.)—
engine—140,000 lb.
booster—13,400 lb.

R.R. Class—Z5

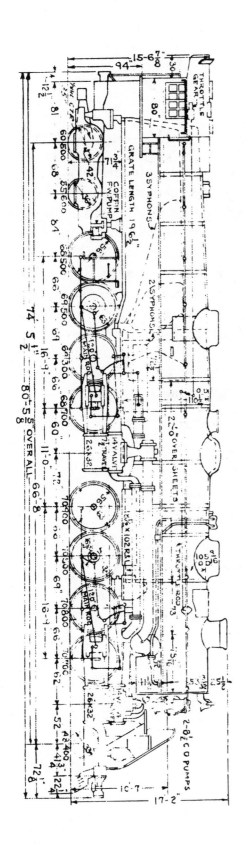

1931

Western Pacific Railroad

NO. 254   2-8-8-2

FROM OROVILLE at the foot of the Sierra Nevada Mountains to Portola, 117 miles away and 4,629 feet higher, the grade is a practically continuous 1 per cent rise. This new route through the Feather River Canyon was completed in 1931 and opened for freight traffic in November. Mallets and Mikados were used on other parts of the Western Pacific but for handling through freight consisting mostly of refrigerator cars carrying California produce, six huge articulateds were ordered. These locomotives rate among the largest and most powerful in existence and can handle without helpers fruit trains of 65 to 74 cars at speeds of 18 to 20 miles an hour over these mountains.

Builder—Baldwin Locomotive Works

Cylinders (4)—26″ x 32″

Weight, total—1,073,350 lb.

Steam Pressure—250 lb.

Fuel—6,000 gal. oil

Water—22,000 gal.

Dia. Drivers—63″

Tractive Effort—
engine—137,000 lb.
booster—13,900 lb.

Nos. 251 to 256

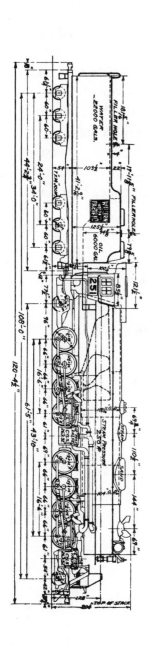

1931

Wabash Railroad

NO. 2921   4-8-4

EIGHTEEN of these Northern-type locomotives went into service late in 1930 and seven in January, 1931, replacing Mountain types to which they were very similar in general design. They were operated in through freight service between Decatur, Illinois, and Montpelier, Ohio, a distance of 272 miles with ruling grades of 0.6 per cent eastbound and 0.9 per cent westbound. The fully enclosed cab is a feature not frequently seen in the United States. Some of these engines were equipped with Timken roller bearings and the tender fuel capacity later increased.

Builder—Baldwin Locomotive
    Works
Cylinders—27″ x 32″
Weight, total—750,600 lb.
Steam Pressure—250 lb.

Fuel—18 tons
Water—15,000 gal.
Dia. Drivers—70″
Tractive Effort—70,817 lb.
R.R. Class—O1
    Nos. 2900 to 2924

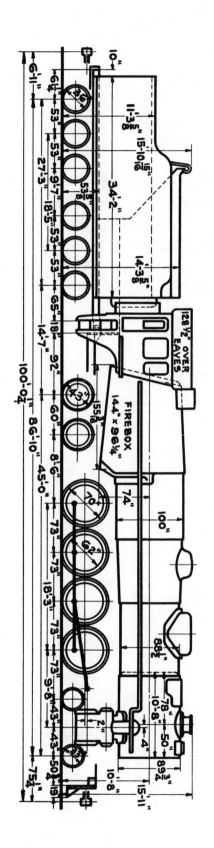

1932

Lehigh Valley Railroad

NO. 5103   4-8-4

THE FIRST of the 4-8-4's (called Wyomings on the "Valley") was the 5100, an experimental locomotive. It was designed to handle a 3,000-ton train on a fast freight schedule over the entire 450-mile main line from Buffalo to Jersey City, including crossing Wilkes Barre Mountain without a helper. The 5100 having fully met requirements, ten similar engines were ordered from Baldwin's, and more built by Alco followed.

Builder—Baldwin Locomotive Works

Cylinders—27″ x 30″

Weight, total—811,500 lb.

Steam Pressure—250 lb.

Fuel—30 tons

Water—20,000 gal.

Dia. Drivers—70″

Tractive Effort—
engine—66,400 lb.
booster—18,360 lb.

R.R. Class—T1

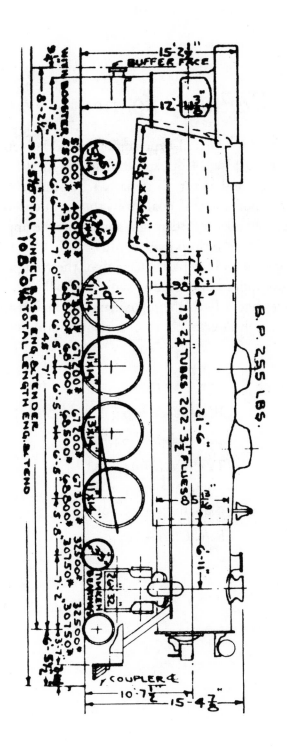

1934

Pittsburgh & West Virginia Railway NO. 1101   2-6-6-4

IN OCTOBER of 1934 three of these articulated-type engines were delivered under their own steam from the Baldwin Eddystone Plant via the Pennsylvania Railroad. The Pittsburgh and West Virginia is a 138-mile road, its main business being the transportation of coal from the Connellsville district of Pennsylvania to the steel mills at Pittsburgh, and across the upper part of West Virginia to Ohio. This new power could handle twice as much tonnage as that formerly used and the particular job of these engines was hauling coal trains the 35½ miles from Connellsville to Rock, Pennsylvania. The three locomotives had a Bethlehem auxiliary engine on the six-wheel rear tender trucks which developed 16,000 pounds additional tractive effort.

Builder—Baldwin Locomotive Works

Cylinders (4)—23″ x 32″

Weight, total—905,640 lb.

Steam Pressure—225 lb.

Fuel—25 tons

Water—20,000 gal.

Dia. Drivers—63″

Tractive Effort—
engine—97,500 lb.
auxiliary—16,000 lb.

R.R. Class—J1

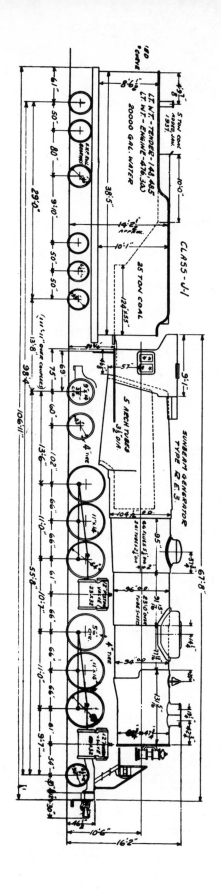

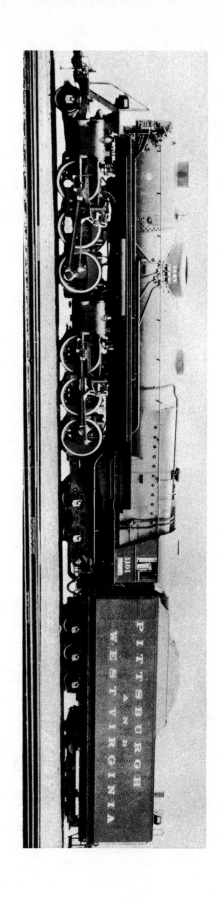

1935

Chicago, Milwaukee, St. Paul & Pacific Railroad

NO. 3   4-4-2

Two NEW high-speed streamlined locomotives were delivered to the Milwaukee Road in May, 1935. They were designed to pull the new Hiawatha on daylight runs between Chicago and the Twin Cities at an average running speed of 66 miles an hour, in six and a half hours. One of the new engines before being placed in regular service made the 141 miles from Milwaukee to New Lisbon in 113 minutes. On the return trip with a train consisting of a dynamometer car and five coaches, it was stopped from a speed of 100 miles an hour in 6,600 feet. The first engines which were followed by two more were finished in the Milwaukee's yellow, orange, maroon, and brown; with all piping and fittings concealed under the shrouding, they presented a very smooth appearance with their clean lines.

Builder—American Locomotive Co.

Cylinders—19" x 28"

Weight, original—527,500 lb. (increased to 563,443 lb.)

Steam Pressure—300 lb.

Fuel—original 4,000 gal. oil (increased to 5,544 gal.)

Water—13,000 gal.

Dia. Drivers—84"

Tractive Effort—30,700 lb.

R.R. Class—A

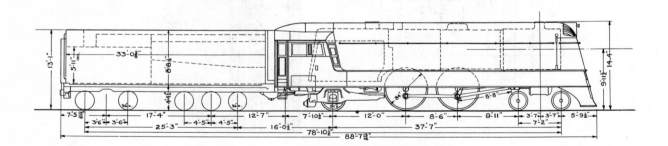

1936

Union Railroad

THE 303 WAS one of the first five locomotives of this wheel arrangement ever built, the type being called Union in honor of the first purchaser. The Union Railroad operates important switching service over 44.75 miles of track in the Pittsburgh district connecting with six trunk-line roads. Previously, six wheel switchers and Consolidations handled the traffic but to eliminate the pusher engines necessary on certain grades, this type of power was designed. Shop and turntable restrictions limited the total wheelbase and as operation was to be at slow speeds, a leading truck was unnecessary; thus with a two-wheeled trailing truck to help carry the weight of the large firebox, the 0-10-2 wheel arrangement resulted. The booster, it will be noted, is applied to the leading tender truck.

Builder—Baldwin Locomotive Works

Cylinders—28″ x 32″

Weight, total—644,510 lb.

Steam Pressure—260 lb.

Fuel—14 tons

Water—12,000 gal.

Dia. Drivers—61″

Tractive Effort—
engine—90,900 lb.
booster—17,150 lb.

Nos. 301 to 303

1936

Norfolk & Western Railway

NO. 1212   2-6-6-4

THESE ARTICULATED locomotives were designed for general use, the first going into service in 1936. By 1944, thirty-five more were in use, and another five were added by 1949. Versatility well describes these engines as they are used for slow freight service in some districts, time freight in others, and for heavy passenger service on practically all the main line. Their slow freight tonnage rating between Williamson, West Virginia, and Portsmouth, Ohio, is 13,000 tons while their time freight tonnage rating between Portsmouth and Columbus is 5,200 tons. In heavy passenger service they are capable of sustained speed in excess of 70 miles an hour. Roller bearings are used throughout on all axles and complete mechanical and pressure lubrication fittings expedite servicing.

Builder—Norfolk & Western

Cylinders (4)—24" x 30"

Weight, total—951,600 lb.

Steam Pressure—300 lb.

Fuel—30 tons

Water—22,000 gal.

Dia. Drivers—70"

Tractive Effort—114,000 lb.

R.R. Class—A

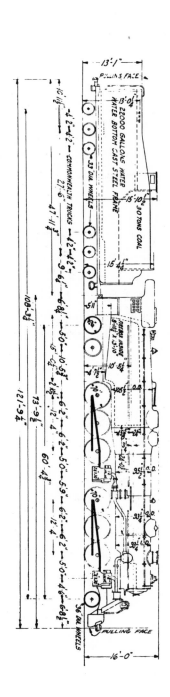

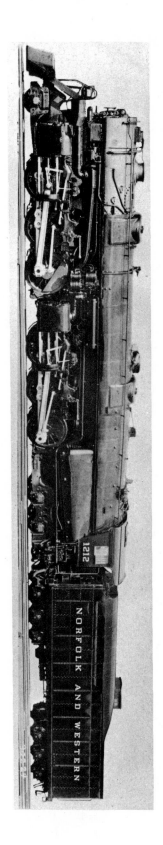

New York, New Haven & Hartford Railroad

NO. 1400   4-6-4

WITH THE increase of passenger traffic on the New Haven's Shore Line requiring trains of fourteen to sixteen cars, the capacity of the I4 Pacifics which had been used for twenty years was severely taxed. As a result of tests with two of these engines with a twelve-car train operating over the 156.8 miles between New Haven and Boston, this new design was worked out. Much research went into these studies, which included consideration of the 0.6 to 0.7 per cent ruling grade near Sharon Heights outside of Boston, and the eventual plans called for a locomotive which could maintain a 60-mile speed over these grades with a twelve-car 830-ton train. Ten of these Class I5 engines were delivered in 1937, being partly streamlined but with maintenance accessibility in mind. They have been satisfactory in every respect since they went into service and will probably remain the last steam locomotives to be purchased by the New Haven.

Builder—Baldwin Locomotive Works

Cylinders—22" x 30"

Weight, total—647,300 lb.

Steam Pressure—285 lb.

Fuel—16 tons

Water—18,000 gal.

Dia. Drivers—80"

Tractive Effort—44,000 lb.

R.R. Class—I5

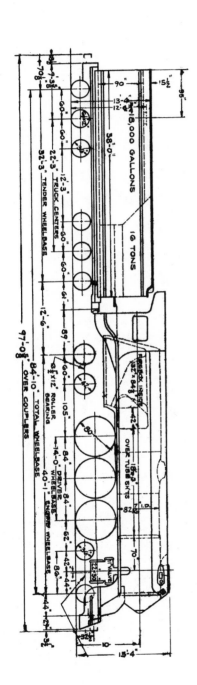

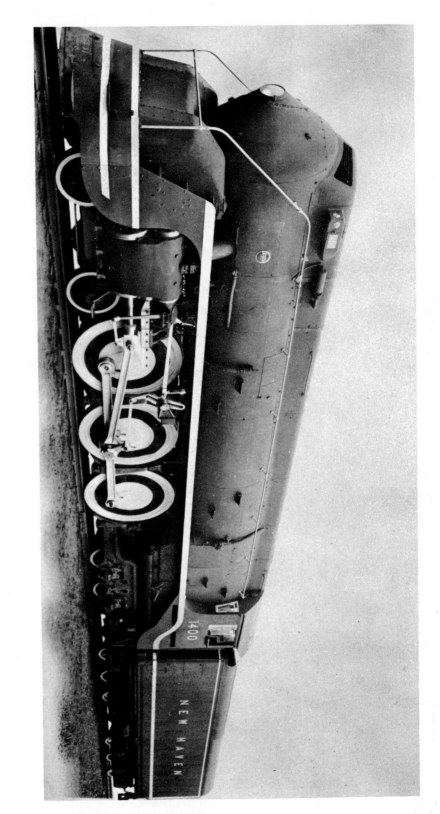

1937

Baltimore & Ohio Railroad

NO. 5600   4-8-4

THE BALTIMORE & OHIO in this locomotive, the George H. Emerson, had another "first"—the original engine having four cylinders with a rigid driving wheelbase. It was the precursor of others to follow, such as the Pennsylvania's four-cylindered types.

Builder—Baltimore & Ohio
Cylinders (4)—18″ x 26½″
Weight, total—689,950 lb.
Steam Pressure—350 lb.

Fuel—23 tons
Water—15,800 gal.
Dia. Drivers—76″
Tractive Effort—65,000 lb.
R.R. Class—N1

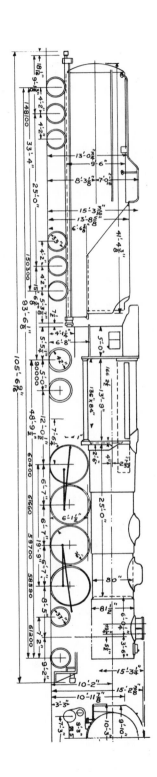

1937

Kansas City Southern Lines

NO. 900 2-10-4

TEN OF THE most powerful Texas types built up to this time made up this order for the Kansas City Southern. Their boiler pressure was the highest yet used in engines of this type. They had a very clean appearance, the piping being placed under the boiler jacket. Five were oil and five were coal burners.

Builder—Lima Locomotive Works

Cylinders—27" x 34"

Weight, total—857,000 lb.

Steam Pressure—310 lb.

Fuel—25 tons or 4,500 gal. oil

Water—20,700 or 21,000 gal.

Dia. Drivers—70"

Tractive Effort—93,300 lb.

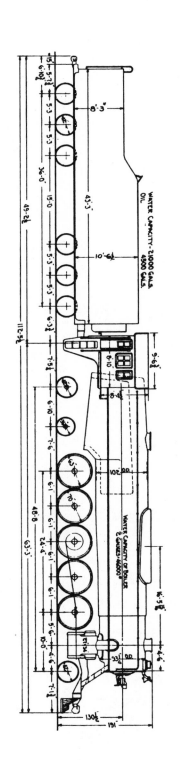

1937

Southern Pacific Railroad   NO. 4439   4-8-4

THE 4439 WAS a later addition to a fleet of 4-8-4 engines, the first of these streamlined types being a group of six which were delivered in 1937. This design met the requirements for locomotives of high tractive power with ability to make high speeds and to handle 600-ton trains over grades. In service they have a schedule which calls for a 9¾ hour run each way between Los Angeles and San Francisco, a distance of 470 miles including a 2.2 per cent grade near Santa Margarita in the Santa Lucia Mountains with some curves up to 10 degrees. The Daylight coach streamliners on which they operate are among the most famous in the world. Powering them and the Larks are the prize assignments of the GS engines although they are also used on several other trains.

Original 4-8-4

Builder—Lima Locomotive Works

Cylinders—27″ x 30″

Weight, total—821,280 lb.

Steam Pressure—250 lb.

Fuel—6,275 gal. oil

Water—22,000 gal.

Dia. Drivers—73½″

Tractive Effort—
engine—62,200 lb.
booster—12,510 lb.

R.R. Class—GS2s

4439

Builder—Lima Locomotive Works

Cylinders—25½″ x 32″

Weight, total—870,600 lb.

Steam Pressure—300 lb.

Fuel—6,275 gal. oil

Water—23,300 gal.

Tractive Effort—
engine—64,800 lb.
booster—13,200 lb.

R.R. Class—GS4s

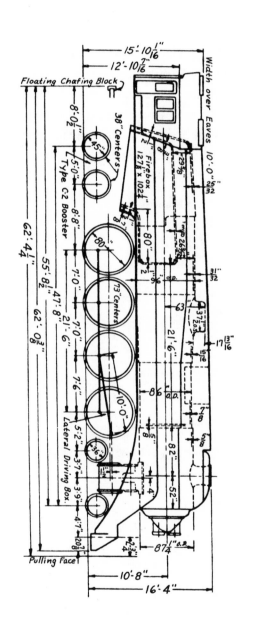

1937

Richmond, Fredericksburg & Potomac Railroad NO. 553 4-8-4

FIVE ENGINES of this design were built for the Capital Cities Route. They were very handsome machines and particular attention was given to their finish and paint work. They were used mainly in freight service and originally averaged fifty-two one-way trips between Richmond and Potomac Yard, often exceeding 5,600 miles a month. The locomotives in this group were named for noted Confederate generals as follows:

No. 551—General Robert E. Lee
No. 552—General T. J. Jackson
No. 553—General J. E. B. Stuart
No. 554—General A. P. Hill
No. 555—General J. E. Johnston

Another group of six very similar locomotives which went into service the following year handling heavy passenger traffic were named for governors of Virginia.

Builder—Baldwin Locomotive Works

Cylinders—27″ x 30″

Weight, total—842,940 lb.

Steam Pressure—275 lb.

Fuel—22 tons

Water—20,000 gal.

Dia. Drivers—77″

Tractive Effort—62,800 lb.

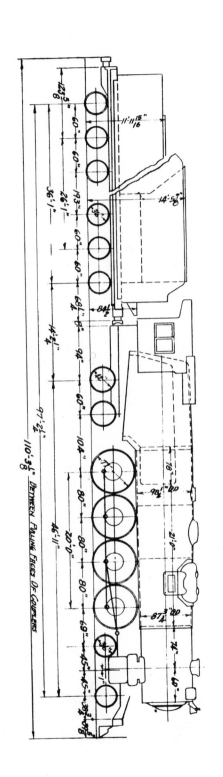

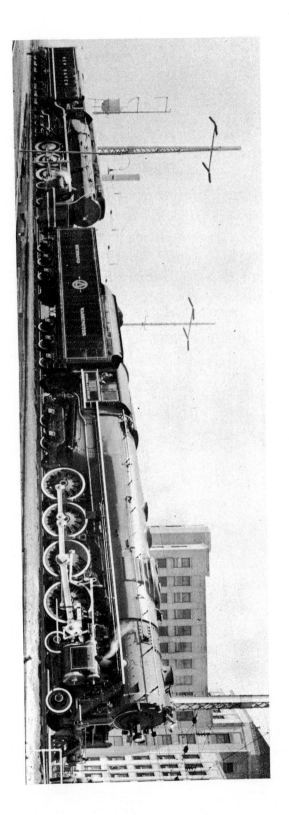

1938

Denver & Rio Grande
Western Railroad   NO. 1801   4-8-4

THIS NORTHERN type was one of five especially designed to handle passenger traffic over the Continental Divide. The ruling grade eastbound from Minturn to Tennessee Pass at the top of the divide is 3.0 per cent and westbound from Pueblo to the pass it is 1.42 per cent. Over this Royal Gorge Route, a distance of 745 miles, these 4-8-4's handled the Western Pacific's crack passenger trains such as the Scenic Limited, operating at speeds up to 80 miles an hour in the Salt Lake district.

Builder—Baldwin Locomotive Works

Cylinders—26″ x 30″

Weight, total—477,360 lb.

Steam Pressure—285 lb.

Fuel—26 tons

Water—20,000 gal.

Dia. Drivers—73″

Tractive Effort—67,200 lb.

R.R. Class—M68

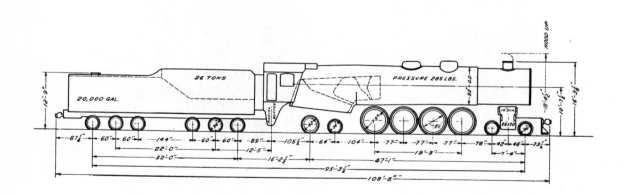

1938

Canadian Pacific Railway

NO. 2850   4-6-4

SIXTY-FIVE of these Hudsons were acquired by the Canadian Pacific to handle high-speed main-line passenger trains. They were semi-streamlined, some had boosters, and the last five were oil burners. When Britain's King and Queen made their tour in 1939, the 2850 was assigned to pull the Royal Train, and it made the entire trip without requiring any adjustments or repairs. The Royal Insignia can be noted on running board and tender.

Builder—Montreal Locomotive Works

Cylinders—22″ x 30″

Weight, total—628,500 lb.

Steam Pressure—275 lb.

Fuel—21 tons

Water—12,000 gal.

Dia. Drivers—75″

Tractive Effort—45,300 lb.

R.R. Class—H1d

Nos. 2800 to 2864

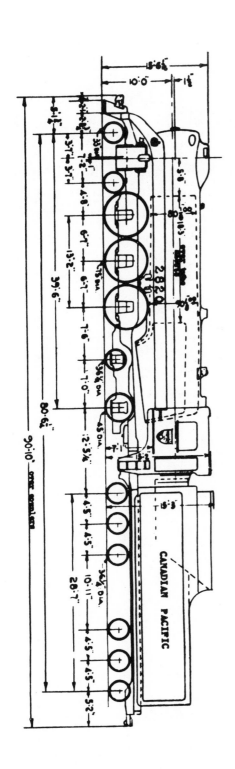

1938

Minneapolis, St. Paul &
Saulte Ste. Marie Railroad NO. 5000 4-8-4

THE FOUR locomotives of this type were the biggest of the steam power owned by the Soo Line. They were used for both freight and passenger service and are the last of the "steamers" the road will have, because of its dieselization program.

Builder—Lima Locomotive
 Works

Cylinders—26" x 32"

Weight, total—771,100 lb.

Steam Pressure—270 lb.

Fuel—24 tons

Water—17,500 gal.

Dia. Drivers—75"

Tractive Effort—
 engine—66,000 lb.
 booster—13,400 lb.

R.R. Class—O20

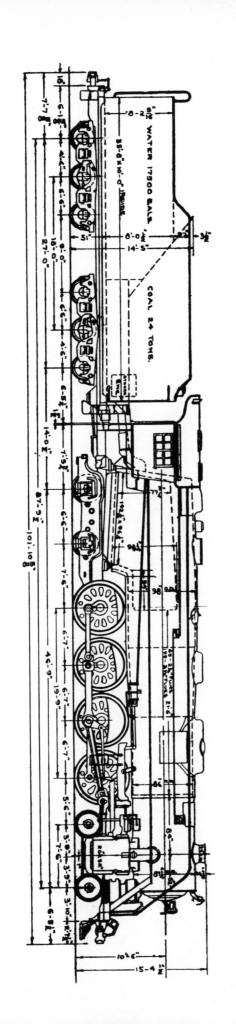

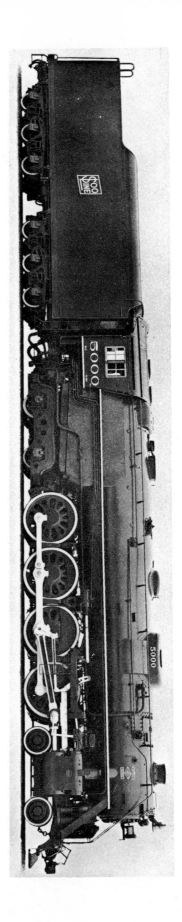

1939

Pennsylvania Railroad

NO. 6100   6-4-4-6

THE S1 WAS the first of the Pennsylvania's several designs of multiple-cylindered locomotives, and at the time of completion was the world's largest and fastest coal-burning passenger engine. It was exhibited at the New York World's Fair in 1939 and 1940 on a special treadmill operating under its own steam. It could handle 1,200-ton trains on the level at 100 miles an hour. It is no longer in existence, having been dismantled in 1949.

Builder—Juniata Shops

Cylinders—22″ x 26″

Weight, total—1,060,000 lb.

Steam Pressure—300 lb.

Fuel—21¼ tons

Water—24,230 gal.

Dia. Drivers—84″

Tractive Effort—71,800 lb.

R.R. Class—S1

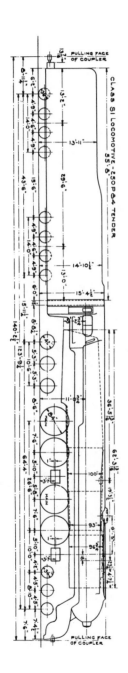

CLASS S1 LOCOMOTIVE - 250 P & 4 TENDER
35'-8"

PULLING FACE
OF COUPLER

PULLING FACE
OF COUPLER

Atchison, Topeka & Santa Fe Railway   NO. 5004   2-10-4

THE FIRST Texas type designed as such for the Santa Fe was the 5000 delivered in December of 1930 and used experimentally. It represented a 50 per cent increase in starting tractive effort over the first series of 2-10-2 type engines of 1903. Following the original 5000, nicknamed the "Madame Queen," ten similar locomotives but with larger drivers were put into service in 1939, and twenty-five more were added to the roster in 1944. All these Texas types are the most powerful non-articulated steam locomotives on the Santa Fe.

Builder—Baldwin Locomotive Works

Cylinders—30" x 34"

Weight, total—880,500 lb.

Steam Pressure—300 lb.

Fuel—27 tons

Water—20,000 gal.

Dia. Drivers—69"

Tractive Effort—93,000 lb.

R.R. Class—5000

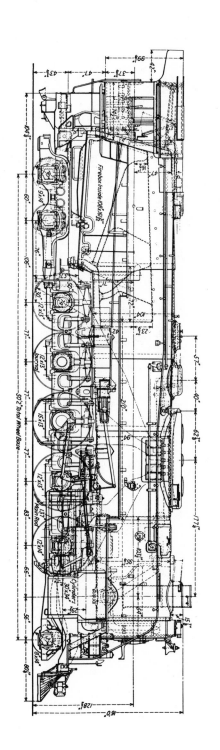

Detroit, Toledo & Ironton Railroad   NO. 704   2-8-4

THE FOUR Berkshire-type locomotives built in 1935 for the D.T. & I. were the first of their wheel arrangement on the road. They were followed by two more in 1939, these making a total of three hundred and two of their type then in service on ten American and Canadian railroads. These were about the smallest 2-8-4's built, considering their tractive power and grate area, although some others totaled more weight.

Builder—Lima Locomotive Works

Cylinders—25″ x 30″

Weight, total—772,370 lb.

Steam Pressure—250 lb.

Fuel—22 tons

Water—22,000 gal.

Dia. Drivers—63″

Tractive Effort—63,250 lb.

R.R. Class—none

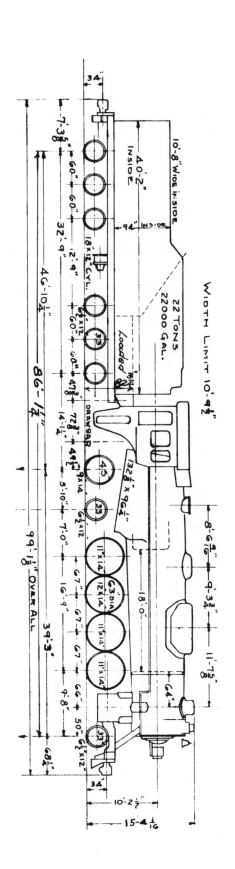

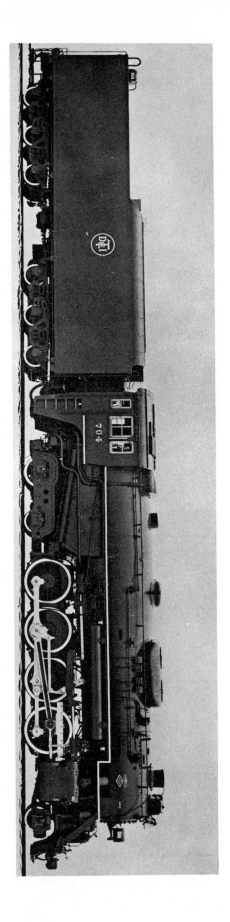

1941

Union Pacific Railroad

NO. 4000   4-8-8-4

THE 4000 IS one of a fleet of twenty-five such locomotives—the largest and heaviest steam motive power in the world. These "Big Boys" have a total length over couplers of 132 feet, 10 inches, and their basic design was developed by engineers of the Research and Mechanical Standards Department of the Union Pacific. Their objective was a locomotive capable of hauling maximum tonnage and maintaining schedules without helpers over the Wasatch Mountains on a ruling grade of 1.14 per cent between Ogden, Utah, and Green River, Wyoming, 176 miles. Tests were made with earlier articulateds and the result was this design, the mechanical details being worked out by Union Pacific engineers and those of the American Locomotive Co. These 4000 series locomotives can operate on any part of the system and can do up to 80 miles an hour, but produce maximum power continuously at 70 miles an hour. They were perhaps the Union Pacific's most important factor in their handling of wartime freight, developing 6,000 drawbar horsepower at 45 miles an hour, and each doing the work of two other locomotives on one of the toughest hauling jobs on any American railroad.

Builder—American Locomotive Co.

Cylinders (4)—23¾" x 32"

Weight, total—1,208,750 lb.

Steam Pressure—300 lb.

Fuel—28 tons

Water—25,000 gal.

Dia. Drivers—68"

Tractive Effort—135,375 lb.

R.R. Class—4000

1941

Norfolk & Western Railway   NO. 600   4-8-4

THE CLASS J locomotives of this type are assigned to handle the principal passenger trains of the Norfolk & Western. Eleven were built from 1941 to 1943, and the first has traveled well over 1,000,000 miles. They have an assignment of from 15,000 to 18,000 miles per locomotive monthly and average 238,000 miles before first shopping is necessary. The longest passenger run they handle is from Roanoke, Virginia, to Cincinnati, Ohio— 424 miles. High mileage is obtained by quick turn-arounds rather than long extended runs. One of these engines has attained a speed of 110 miles an hour handling a fifteen-car, 1,025-ton train on level tangent track.

Builder—Norfolk & Western   *Fuel*—35 tons

Cylinders—27″ x 32″   *Water*—20,000 gal.

Weight, total—872,600 lb.   *Dia. Drivers*—70″

Steam Pressure—300 lb.   *Tractive Effort*—80,000 lb.

                                      R.R. Class—J

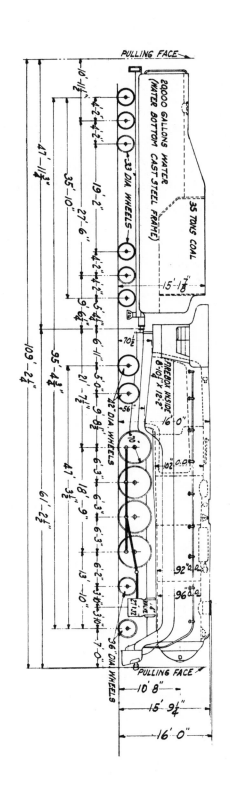

PULLING FACE

20000 GALLONS WATER
(WATER BOTTOM CAST STEEL FRAME)

35 TONS COAL

33 DIA. WHEELS

42" DIA. WHEELS

FIREBOX INSIDE
8'-10½" X 12'-2"

36 DIA. WHEELS

PULLING FACE

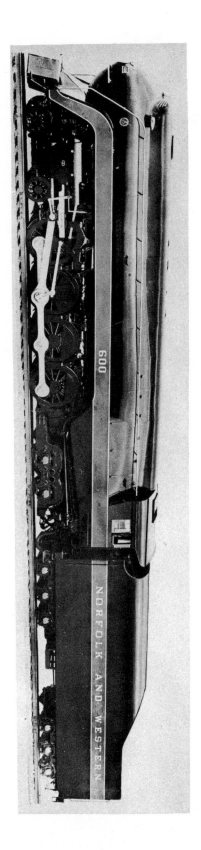

600

NORFOLK AND WESTERN

Chesapeake & Ohio Railway   NO. 1625   2-6-6-6

THE FIRST of the C. & O.'s Allegheny types appeared a few months earlier than the 1625—in December, 1941. They were (and are) a most successful design of articulated, so satisfactory, in fact, that repeat orders up to 1949 have resulted. They were at that time the largest locomotives built by Lima. In service they handle 5,750 tons over the grades between Clifton Forge, Virginia, and Hinton, West Virginia, unassisted.

Builder—Lima Locomotive Works

Cylinders (4)—22½″ x 33″

Weight, total—1,098,540 lb.

Steam Pressure—260 lb.

Fuel—25 tons

Water—25,000 gal.

Dia. Drivers—67″

Tractive Effort—110,200 lb.

R.R. Class—H8

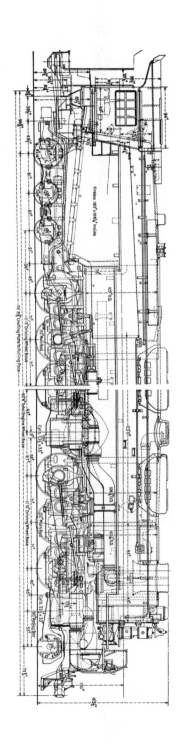

Pennsylvania Railroad

NO. 6474   2-10-4

THIS heavy-duty freight power represents in most respects a departure from usual Pennsylvania standards. Early in World War II when the problem of additional motive power for all the country's railroads was being worked out, the Pennsylvania was practically assigned Texas types for freight handling. The design is based on the C. & O.'s engines of 1930, then described as the largest and most powerful two-cylindered locomotives in the world. Pennsylvania modifications are the very large tender and special cabs, as well as a number of other changes, but the usual Belpaire firebox is conspicuously absent. The first of one hundred and twenty-five of these engines went into service in December, 1942, and the rest followed through the next year. They were an important factor in expediting the movement of wartime freight and have proved very satisfactory, now being in service on most divisions.

Builder—Altoona Shops

Cylinders—29" x 54"

Weight, total—977,380 lb.

Steam Pressure—270 lb.

Fuel—29⁹⁄₁₀ tons

Water—21,000 gal.

Dia. Drivers—69"

Tractive Effort—
  engine—95,100 lb.
  booster—15,000 lb.

R.R. Class—J1, J1a

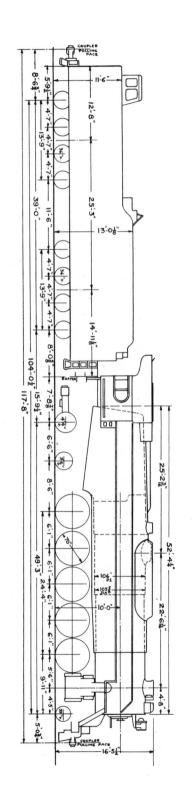

St. Louis, Southwestern Railway   NO. 815   4-8-4

THE 815 is one of five locomotives which were designed and constructed by the Cotton Belt's own staff of mechanical engineers, foremen, and shopmen at their shops at Pine Bluff, Arkansas. The original 4-8-4's on the road were a group of ten built by Baldwin's in 1930, and these were followed by five more in 1937. Designed for handling fast freight, these L1's were numbered 815 to 819.

Builder—St. Louis, Southwestern   *Fuel*—5,000 gal. oil

Cylinders—26" x 30"   *Water*—15,000 gal.

Weight, total—750,500 lb.   *Dia. Drivers*—70"

Steam Pressure—250 lb.   *Tractive Effort*—61,564 lb.

     R.R. Class—L1

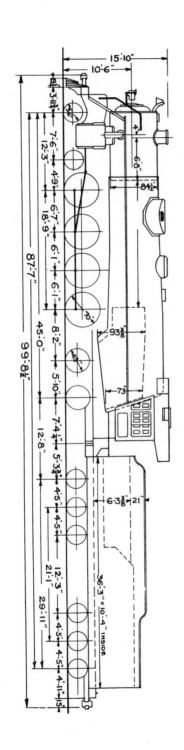

1942

Louisville & Nashville Railroad   NO. 1960   2-8-4

FOURTEEN of these Berkshires, the first of their type the L. & N. had ever had, were put into service late in 1942; these were supplemented by six more in 1944 and still another twenty-two up to 1949. Having larger drivers and greater boiler capacity than the Mikados they replaced, their tractive force at higher speeds is considerably greater. These 2-8-4's have "everything" from roller bearings to booster and are as completely modern as steam motive power can be.

Builder—Baldwin Locomotive
    Works (Nos. 1950 to 1969)

Cylinders—25″ x 32″

Weight, total—831,400 lb.

Steam Pressure—265 lb.

Fuel—25 tons

Water—22,000 gal.

Dia. Drivers—69″

Tractive Effort—
    engine—65,290 lb.
    booster—14,100 lb.

R.R. Class—M1

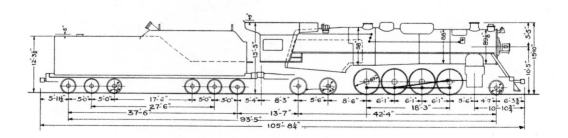

Northern Pacific Railway   NO. 5139   4-6-6-4

PIONEERED BY the Union Pacific in 1936 and also first put into service the same year by the Northern Pacific, the 4-6-6-4 type of articulateds immediately proved their versatility and capabilities. The 5139 was one of a repeat order for twenty built through 1943 and 1944. Although dual service locomotives, this class is used principally for heavy freight traffic in districts with heavy ruling grades. All are roller bearing equipped on all axles.

Builder—American Locomotive Co.

Cylinders (4)—23″ x 32″

Weight, total—1,081,000 lb.

Steam Pressure—260 lb.

Fuel—27 tons

Water—25,000 gal.

Dia. Drivers—70″

Tractive Effort—106,890 lb.

R.R. Class—Z8

Nos. 5130 to 5149

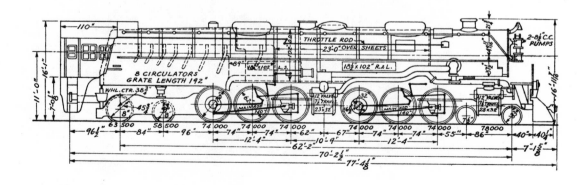

1943

Central of Georgia Railway

NO. 455   4-8-4

A NUMBER OF well-known Chicago-to-Florida through passenger trains are handled over the trackage of the Central of Georgia; among them are the Southland, Dixie Flyer, Dixie Limited, Flamingo, Seminole, and City of Miami. To better handle these, as well as fast freight, eight 4-8-4's were purchased at a cost of $178,000 each. These locomotives can maintain fast schedules between Macon and Atlanta with twenty-two passenger cars northbound or thirty cars southbound and have about 25 per cent more tractive power than the Mountain-type engines they replaced.

Builder—Lima Locomotive
    Works

Cylinders—27" x 30"

Weight, total—643,700 lb.

Steam Pressure—250 lb.

Fuel—21 tons

Water—13,000 gal.

Dia. Drivers—73"

Tractive Effort—63,200 lb.

Nos. 451 to 458

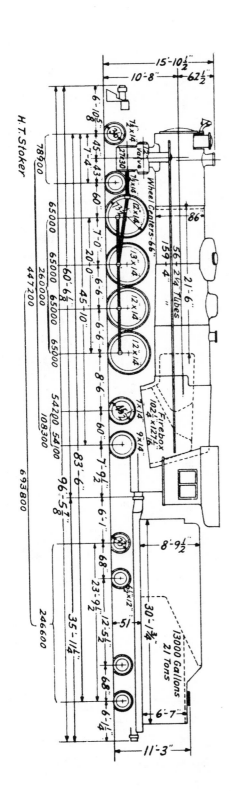

1944

Pennsylvania Railroad

NO. 6200   6-8-6

THIS YEAR marked a particular milestone for steam in that the Pennsylvania placed in service the first coal-burning locomotive without cylinders—the S2, first direct-drive steam turbine engine ever built in the United States. Jointly designed by Baldwin, Westinghouse, and Pennsylvania engineers, it had two turbines for forward and reverse operation. Some of the objectives of the design were to eliminate the reciprocating parts of the conventional steam engine, obtain a uniform application of power to the drivers, and gain the economies turbo-drive makes possible—at speeds above 30 miles an hour, steam consumption per horsepower at the rail is considerably less than that of a comparable reciprocating steam locomotive. Maximum efficiency is reached at a speed of about 70 miles an hour, although with a full-length standard train it can attain a 100-mile-an-hour speed.

Builder—Baldwin Locomotive Works

Forward turbine—6,900 H.P. at operating speed of 9,000 R.P.M.

Reverse turbine—1,500 H.P. at operating speed of 8,300 R.P.M.

Weight, total—1,040,200 lb.

Steam Pressure—310 lb.

Length, coupler to coupler—122 feet 7¼ inches

Fuel—42½ tons

Water—19,500 gal.

Dia. Drivers—68"

Tractive Effort—
forward—70,500 lb.
reverse—65,000 lb.

R.R. Class—S2

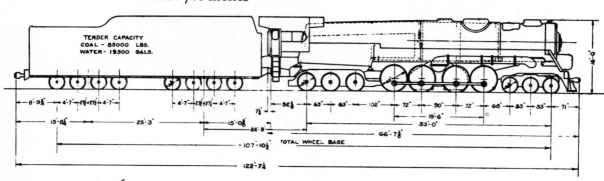

Baltimore & Ohio Railroad   NO. 7600   2-8-8-4

ONE OF THE latest and most advanced designs of articulated locomotives is this Class EM1 on the Baltimore & Ohio. While they are not as powerful or heavy as some other engines of this wheel arrangement because of definite weight specifications, they are, nevertheless, the heaviest on the B. & O. The design was worked out by Baldwin's in collaboration with the Motive Power Department and the first ten ordered were received in February, 1944. Followed by twenty more by September, 1945, they filled an important assignment handling freight over the Cumberland Division. The record-breaking tonnage moved over the Seventeen Mile Grade and Cranberry and Cheat River Grades toward the closing months of the war was handled largely and most efficiently by the EM1's.

Builder—Baldwin Locomotive Works

Cylinders (4)—24″ x 32″

Weight, total—1,010,700 lb.

Steam Pressure—235 lb.

Fuel—25 tons

Water—22,000 gal.

Dia. Drivers—64″

Tractive Effort—115,000 lb.

R.R. Class—EM1

Nos. 7600 to 7619 (1944)
7620 to 7629 (1945)

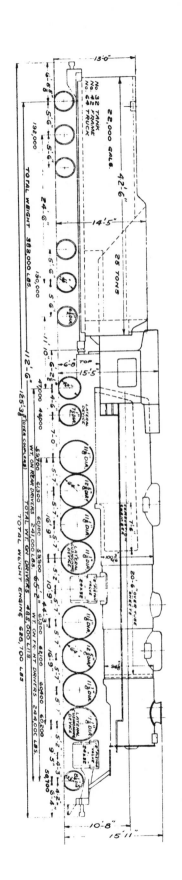

1944

Pennsylvania Railroad

IN 1942 THE Pennsylvania Railroad, as a result of studies originated with the S1 (page 215), built an experimental 4-6-4-4-type locomotive having four cylinders, two being opposed under the firebox, a rigid main frame, and 77″ driving wheels. After extensive road tests with this 6130, the 4-4-6-4 type resulted—reversing the former's wheel arrangement and with both pairs of cylinders ahead of smaller drivers. It represents the most radical departure from conventional steam-locomotive design to be put into production since the appearance of the simple articulated engine, twenty-six of the class having been built. They are used in freight service and can make up to 70-mile-an-hour speeds.

Builder—Altoona Shops

Cylinders (2)—19¾″ x 28″
         (2)—23¾″ x 29″

Weight, total—1,041,000 lb.

Steam Pressure—300 lb.

Fuel—37½ tons

Water—19,200 gal.

Dia. Drivers—69″

Tractive Effort—
    engine—100,800 lb.
    booster—15,000 lb.

R.R. Class—Q2

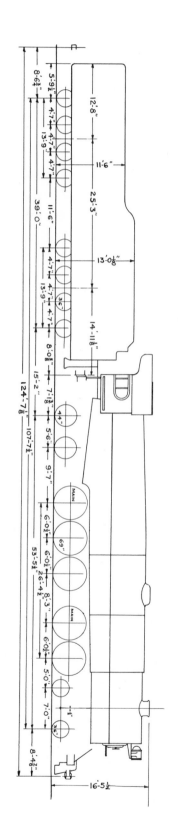

1945

Western Maryland Railway   NO. 6   4-4-4 Shay-geared

LAST OF the Shay-geared locomotives was this Western Maryland representative. Such engines had a wide range of operation—for industrial, logging, mining, quarry, and contractors' use. Some, however, have been used for special service where standard locomotives were impractical on trunk-line roads such as the New York Central (on Tenth Avenue in Manhattan before grade separation), the Chesapeake & Ohio, and the Western Maryland.

Builder—Lima Locomotive
    Works

Cylinders (3)—17″ x 18″

Weight, total—324,000 lb.

Steam Pressure—200 lb.

Fuel—9 tons

Water—6,000 gal.

Dia. Drivers—48″

Tractive Effort—59,740 lb.

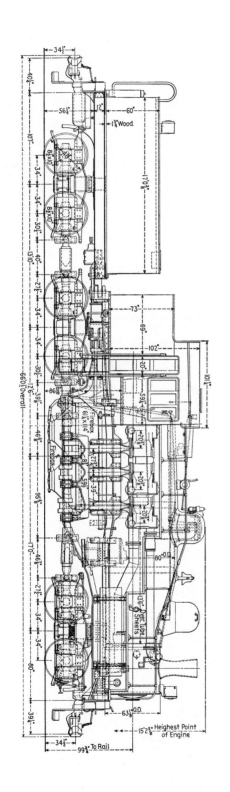

1945

Reading Company

NO. 2100   4-8-4

LATEST OF Reading steam power are the thirty 4-8-4's of this type, the first eight being completed in 1945. The design was worked out by Baldwin's and the Reading Motive Power Department and the engines were built at the Reading Shops. They are used principally in freight service, where their performance has been excellent.

Builder—Reading Company

Cylinders—27″ x 32″

Weight, total—809,000 lb.

Steam Pressure—240 lb.

Fuel—26 tons

Water—19,000 gal.

Dia. Drivers—70″

Tractive Effort—
engine—68,000 lb.
booster—11,100 lb.

R.R. Class—T1

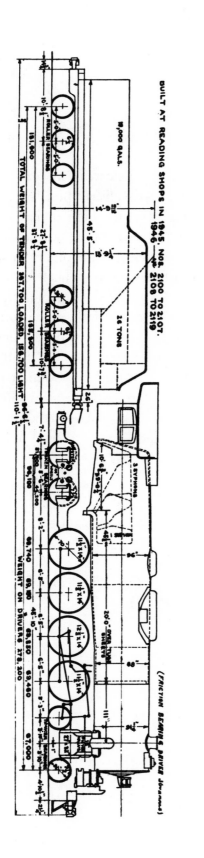

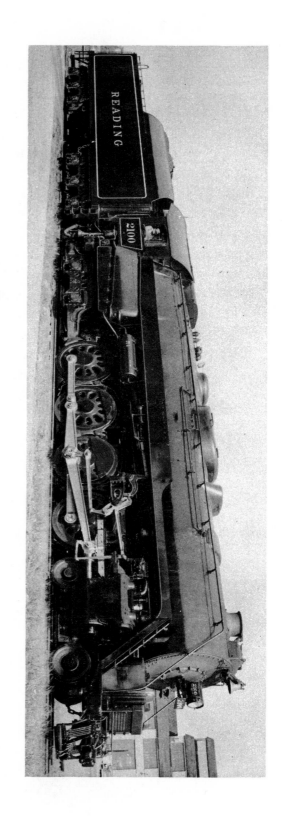

1945

Pennsylvania Railroad

NO. 5505   4-4-4-4

Two LOCOMOTIVES of this type were built by Baldwin's in 1942 and operated experimentally in main-line service as well as upon the Altoona Test Plant. The 5505 was one of another fifty, the biggest fleet of four-cylinder rigid-frame locomotives, built as the result of the satisfactory performance of the first two. They are direct descendants of the S1 in general characteristics except that instead of having six-wheel leading and trailing trucks, these are four-wheel, and a different streamlining treatment has been applied. The tenders are the second largest ever built and permit runs of 713 miles from Harrisburg to Chicago with only one coaling stop at Millbrook, Ohio. Poppet valves, roller bearings throughout, including rods and crossheads and forced feed oil lubrication at eighty-eight points, were factors contributing to 93 to 94 per cent machine efficiency registered on tests. The T1's were designed to handle 880-ton trains at 100 miles an hour on level track and have been used in heaviest passenger service until superseded by diesels.

Builder—Baldwin Locomotive Works (27) Altoona Shops (25)

Cylinders (4)—18¾" x 26"

Weight, total—953,370 lb.

Steam Pressure—300 lb.

Length, coupler to coupler—122 feet 9¾ inches

Fuel—41 tons

Water—19,500 gal.

Dia. Drivers—80"

Tractive Effort—64,650 lb.

R.R. Class—T1

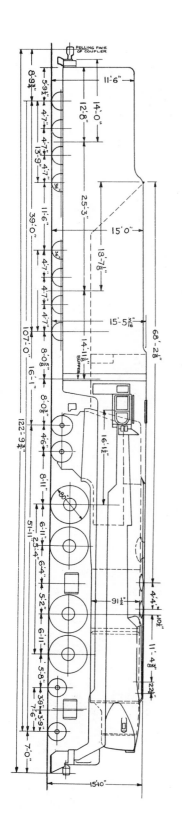

1946

New York Central Railroad　　　NO. 6001　　4-8-4

THE TWENTY-FIVE Niagaras of this type were almost the last steam locomotives to be purchased by the New York Central. Built in 1945 and
1946, the S1's were designed as dual-purpose engines but they have been
used almost exclusively in passenger service. These Niagaras have set an
unprecedented record in flexibility and economy of operation and have
made the highest records for mileage and availability of any steam locomotives in the world.

Builder—American Locomotive
　Co.

Cylinders—25½″ x 32″

Weight, engine—471,000 lb.

Steam Pressure—290 lb.

Fuel—46 tons

Water—18,000 gal.

Dia. Drivers—79″

Tractive Effort—61,570 lb.

R.R. Class—S1

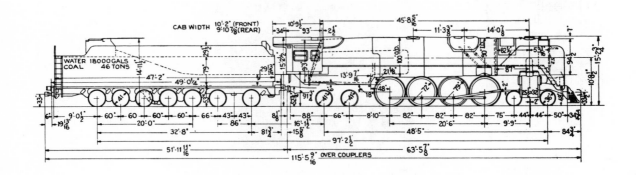

1947

Chesapeake & Ohio Railway   NO. 500   4-8-8-4 Turbo-Electric

THE 500 IS one of three such locomotives—the world's first steam turbine electrics. In these machines, the coal compartment is forward and from this a mechanical stoker feeds coal into the firebox which, with a conventional boiler, occupies the center section. At the rear is the 6,000 H.P. turbine and two 2,000 K.W. generators which supply the electric current for driving the eight axle-hung motors. Back of the locomotive is the tender, which carries only water. A total length of 154 feet makes this the longest steam locomotive ever built and it is the heaviest as well. It is completely streamlined, roller bearing equipped, has electrically operated brakes as well as air brakes, and can make speeds up to 100 miles an hour. Like so many locomotives, it gained a nickname almost immediately—the "Sacred Cow."

Builder—Baldwin Locomotive Works

Turbine—6,000 H.P.

Generators (2)—2,000 K.W. each

Motors (8)—580 volt

Weight, total—1,233,970 lb.

Steam Pressure—310 lb.

Fuel—29¼ tons

Water—25,000 gal.

Dia. Drivers—40″

Tractive Effort—98,000 lb.

R.R. Class—M1

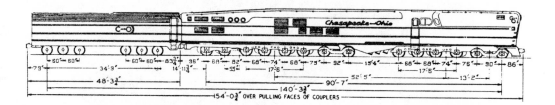

1948

Norfolk & Western Railway   NO. 2156   2-8-8-2

THE FIRST of this type of freight motive power on the Norfolk and Western was built in 1930 (Y5) and others (Y6 and Y6a) followed up to 1948, seventeen (Y6b) being built that year. Where conditions permit, these articulateds can handle tonnage trains at speeds up to 45 or 50 miles an hour. They are used particularly for hauling coal on the heavy grades of the Pocahontas, Radford, and Shenandoah Divisions. These are the most recent of true Mallet locomotives as they are all compounds.

Builder—Norfolk & Western

Cylinders (2 H.P.)—25″ x 32″
          (2 L.P.)—39″ x 32″

Weight, total—961,500 lb.

Steam Pressure—300 lb.

Fuel—30 tons

Water—22,000 gal.

Dia. Drivers—58″

Tractive Effort—
    simple—152,206 lb.
    compound—126,838 lb.

R.R. Class—Y6a

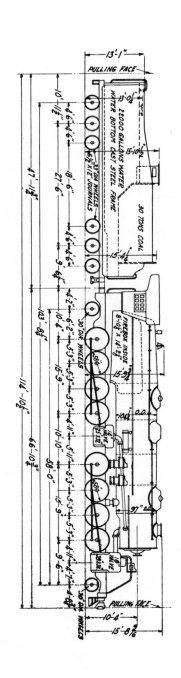

1949

New York, Chicago &
St. Louis Railroad

NO. 776   2-8-4

BESIDES BEING the last word in Berkshire types, the Nickel Plate and Louisville & Nashville 2-8-4's were actually the last steam locomotives to be built commercially, as distinguished from those built by railroad shops. The L. & N. order was for twenty-two engines, the same as those purchased in 1942, and the last to be shipped was No. 1991 on May 11, 1949. The last Nickel Plate locomotive, one of ten, the No. 779, has the distinction of being the last steam engine for domestic use to leave the Lima plant, this being shipped May 13, 1949. Both Berkshire types are completely modern freight power and probably the "last of their race."

Builder—Lima-Hamilton Corp.

Cylinders—25″ x 34″

Weight, total—808,910 lb.

Steam Pressure—245 lb.

Fuel—22 tons

Water—22,000 gal.

Dia. Drivers—69″

Tractive Effort—64,100 lb.

R.R. Class—S3

Nos. 770 to 779

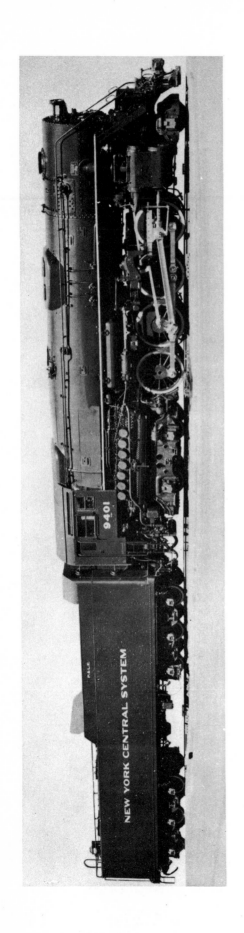